Enjoy The Sound Of

Pump it up

RADIO

Get the free Pump it up magazine Radio App on your smartphone or tablet, and you'll never miss your favourite music !

POP - ROCK - DANCE - RNB - JAZZ
Available on Google Play Store

www.PumpItUpMagazine.com

Pump it up Magazine

TABLE OF CONTENTS

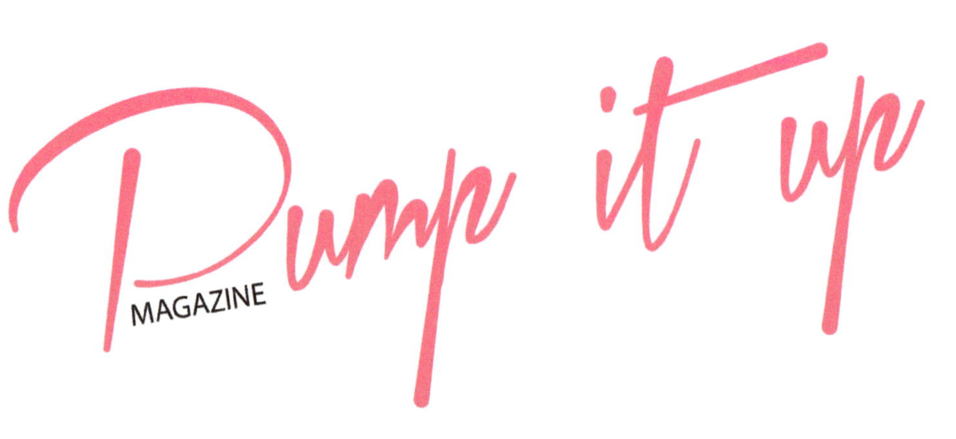

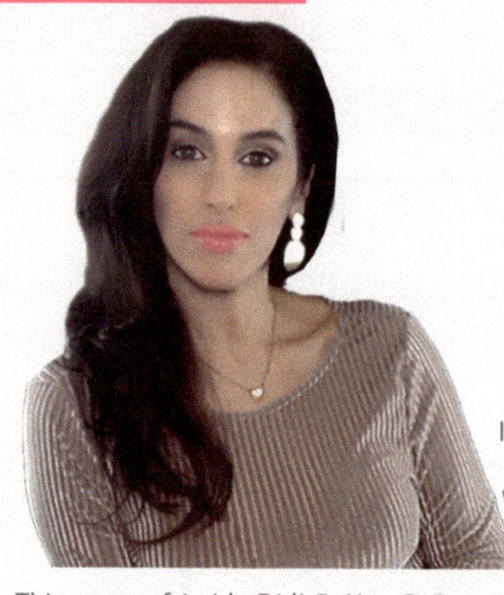

Greetings,

I hope every one of our readers is enjoying this long hot summer. It's been hotter than usual so please make sure to stay hydrated and cool.

In this months edition, we have on the cover girl group "Rumble G".
With the emergence and popularity of k-Pop

This group of 4 girls, Didi Ga Yun, BaRum, and IAn are ready to take on the world with their debut single" Rootpretelcham"
So dive in and read more about the next big K-Pop sensation " Rumble G".

And we approach the day of Michael Jackson's passing we invite you to read a short article to remind you that The King of Pop was a a special person and a good human being. Gone too soon.

On page 17 is a great article on Girl groups around the world.
Can you guess which is the biggest selling girl group in history?

(not gonna tell) I'll give you a hint..Sugar and S____________ and everything nice!
That's what girls are made of.

And we move on in our expose of Girl Groups, we introduce you to some girl groups from around the world you may not have been aware of.

Check out some of our hottest new indie artist's,
And my top tips, one of the main reason I created this magazine,
to support and help indie artists!

If you need to know more about this music business from an indie artist standpoint then you will want to pick up or order a copy of The Modern Artist Handbook by Bernie Capodici. A good and educational read.

Being that I am French and my husband is
American, we have teamed up to introduce a series of children's books (adults too) learn French and English in a fun and entertaining way.

So flip through the pages and see even more on Music, Film, Fashion the arts and more.

And don't forget to tune in to Pump it Up Magazine Radio for your daily dose of the best of indie and mainstream artists.

Anissa Boudjaoui

CONTRIBUTORS

EDITOR IN CHIEF
Anissa Boudjaoui

MUSIC
Michael B. Sutton
A. Scott Galloway
Sarah Kaye

FASHION
Tiffani Sutton

MARKETING
Grace Rose

PARTNERS

Editions L.A.
www.editions-la.com

The Sound Of L.A.
www.thesoundofla.com

Info Music
www.infomusic.fr

Delit Face
www.DelitFace.com

L.A. Unlimited
www.launlimitedinc.com

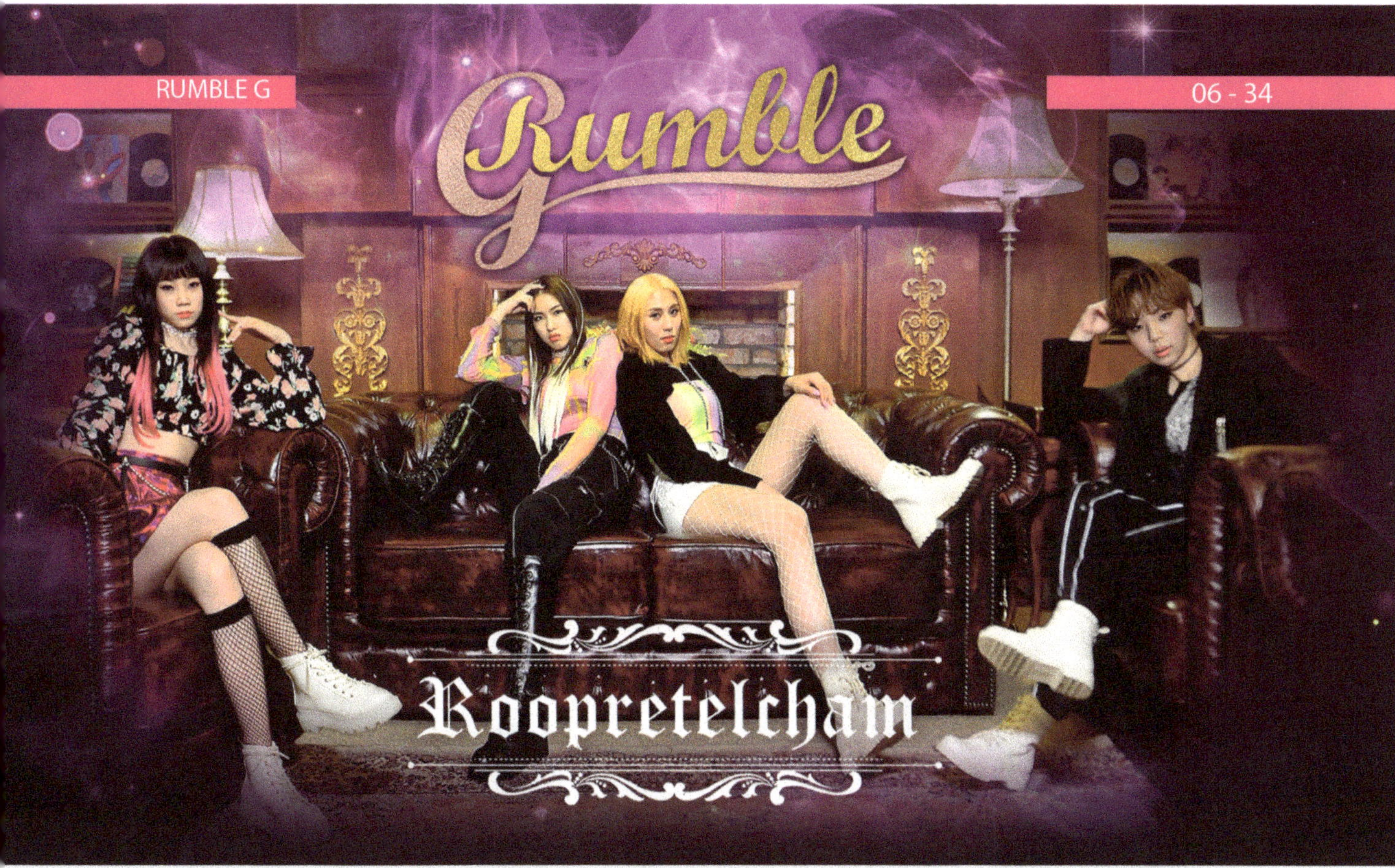

With their collective interest, incredible talent, and extensive experience growing up with a passionate desire to entertain, K-Pop's new sensation Rumble-G are set to dominate the charts in their breakout year. Combining the extraordinary singing voices, personalities & skillsets of DiDi (Leader/Rap/Vocals), GaYun (Dance/Vocals), BaRum (Vocals), and IAn (Rap/Vocals) – together they're a verifiable force in the international music-scene with an extremely bright future ahead as they surge into their unified career.

Ready to turn their wildest dreams into their daily reality and a lifetime immersed in music that they can share with each and every one of YOU listening & watching their videos online from around the globe – Rumble-G contains an exciting level of balance between what their individual styles & sounds, leading to a cohesive and empowered all-girl group that is capable of exceeding their amazing potential & reaching the hearts & minds of millions all over the world.

From their remarkable voices & stunning personalities to their electrifying abilities as dancers & pure entertainers, Rumble-G has all the essential ingredients of modern-day K-Pop, with an unrivalled enthusiasm & desire to make music that sets them apart from any other in all the right ways. Destined to be number one and be leaders in the scene for the rest to follow –

Rumble-G is a complete revelation in hybrid K-Pop, & 100% absolutely irresistible from sight to sound.

Making their official debut in 2021 with their first single "Rootpretelcham," a visually gorgeous & all-out cinematic video supporting it, and a wonderfully devout fan-base listening & watching their every move online through social media – Rumble-G has gone on to rack up hundreds of thousands of clicks & views, with no signs of their single slowing down anytime soon as it catches fire and thrives across the internet.

Join DiDi, GaYun, BaRum & IAn, in their groundbreaking debut year as they dominate playlists with their new single "Rootpretelcham" & win their way into the hearts & homes of listeners all around the world by making music with dazzling sincerity, radiant melodies, and undeniable energy designed to move you.

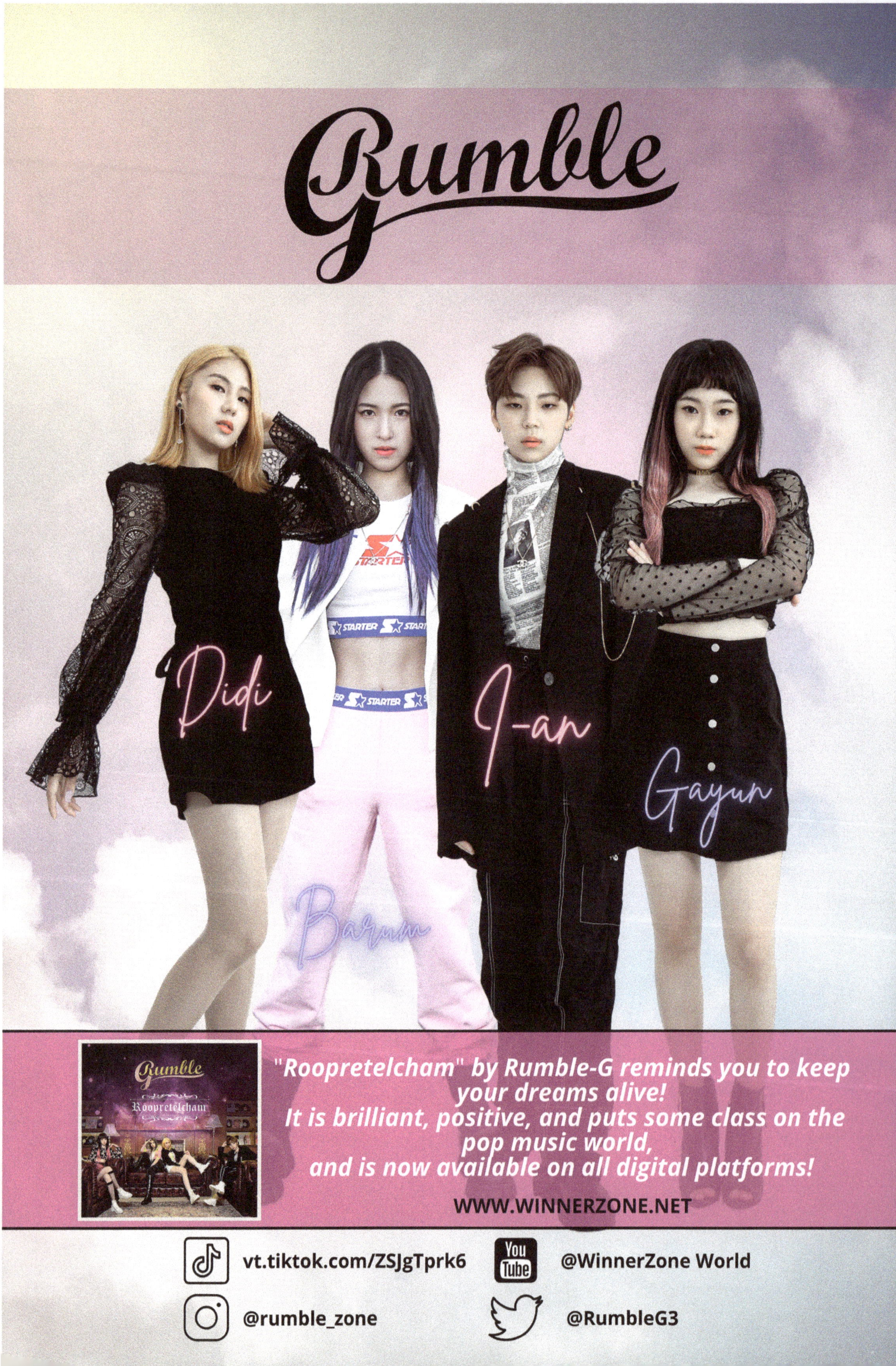

Rumble

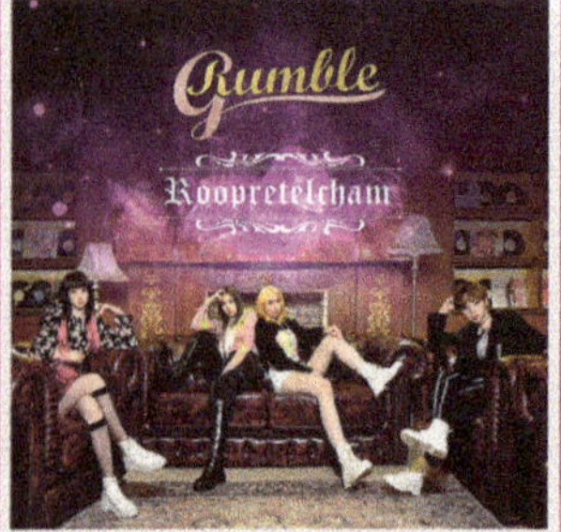

"Roopretelcham" by Rumble-G reminds you to keep your dreams alive!
It is brilliant, positive, and puts some class on the pop music world,
and is now available on all digital platforms!

WWW.WINNERZONE.NET

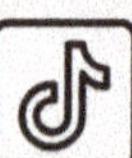 vt.tiktok.com/ZSJgTprk6

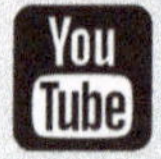 @WinnerZone World

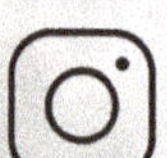 @rumble_zone

 @RumbleG3

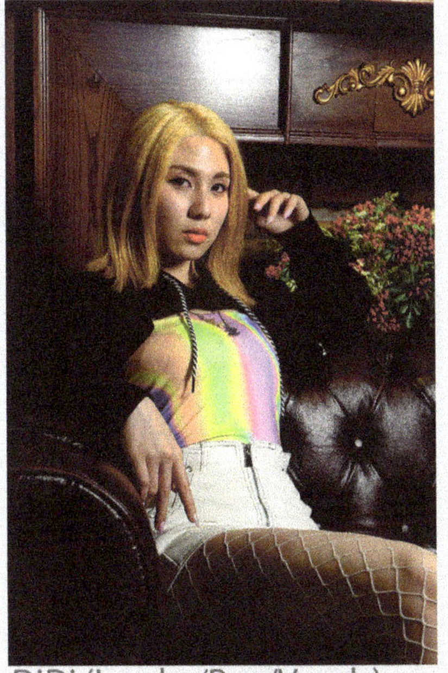

DiDi (Leader/Rap/Vocals)

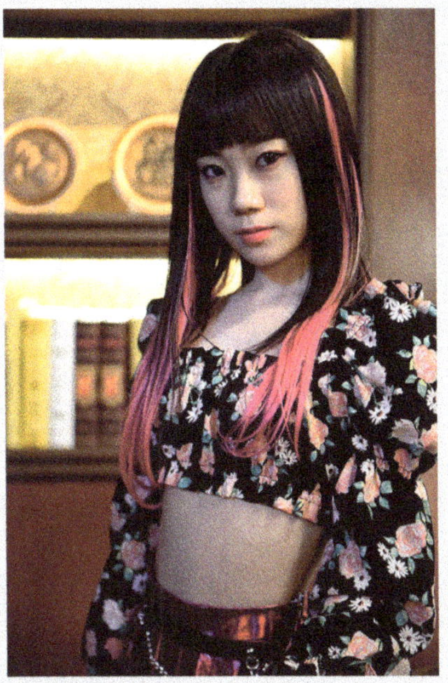

GaYun (Dance/Vocals)

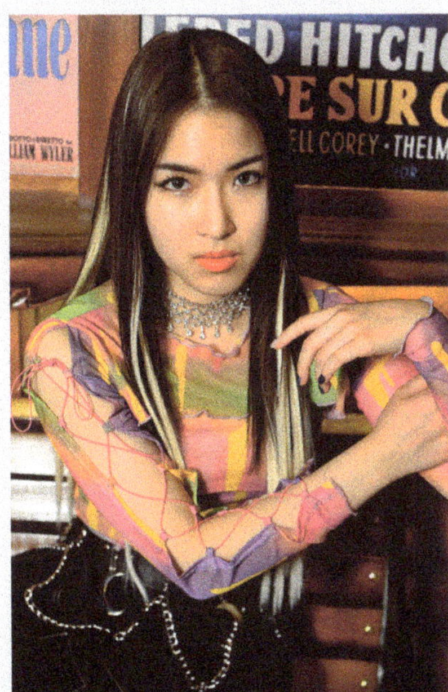

BaRum (Vocals)

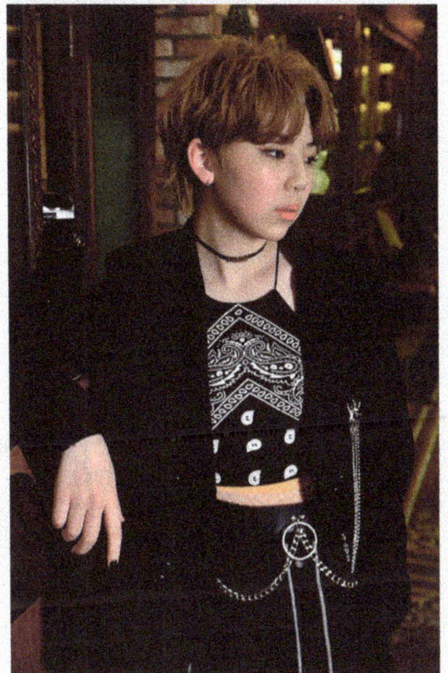

IAn (Rap/Vocals)

1. GREAT TO HAVE YOU ON PUMP IT UP MAGAZINE. PLEASE, INTRODUCE YOURSELF?

Great to be here! We are DiDi (Leader/Rap/Vocals), GaYun (Dance/Vocals), BaRum (Vocals), and IAn (Rap/Vocals) – together, we are Rumble G., formed by WinnerZone Entertainment!

2. HOW DID YOU GET STARTED IN THE MUSIC BUSINESS?

We naturally came across music as we have dreamed of becoming a musician since we were young.

3. TELL US ABOUT YOUR NEW SINGLE ROOPRETELCHAM,

Roopretelcham is a magic spell meaning "may all of your wishes come true" in Latin. We want spread positivity and motivate everybody to not to give up on their dreams and wishes.

4. WHAT MAKES YOUR PRODUCTIONS UNIQUE? AND HOW WOULD YOU DESCRIBE IT?

Our new single "Ropertelcham is very unique because it will certainly capture your attention right from the start!
|This track draws from various elements; including r&b and hip-hop but is primarily based in electronic dance music (EDM). The song carries a motivational theme of achieving one's dreams, which puts a tasteful layer of musicality on this thunderous rhythm!

5. WHO ARE YOUR BIGGEST MUSICAL INFLUENCES? AND ANY PARTICULAR ARTIST/BAND YOU WOULD LIKE TO COLLABORATE WITH IN THE FUTURE?

There are various musicians and artists that we love and get our inspiration from. Among them, our one pick is Little Mix . Because we love their energy on stage while performing and their

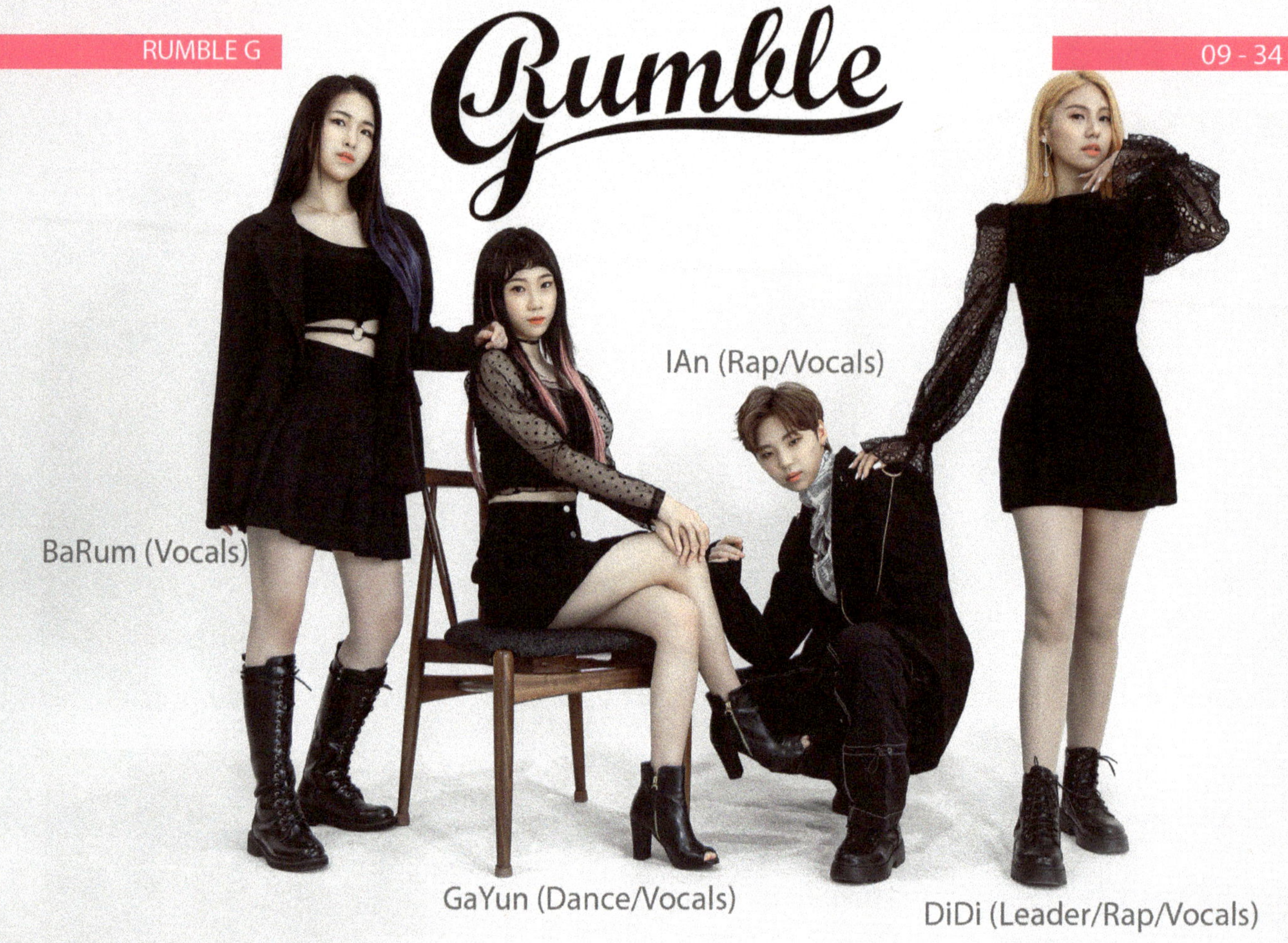

6. IF YOU HAD ONE MESSAGE TO GIVE TO YOUR FANS, WHAT WOULD IT BE?

REMEMBER YOUR DREAMS!! Don't forget to achieve them, stay positive! Have faith, because dreams come true!!!
We are so thankful for the love and support of our fans!You guys give us the biggest and great strength. We hope to meet you guys in person as soon as possible

7. WHICH IS THE BEST MOMENT IN YOUR MUSICAL CAREER THAT YOU'RE MOST PROUD OF?

Our proudest moment is now, it is what we have achieve so far, releasing a single, a super cool music video it is on YouTube and will be on many other platforms, and already has so many views, we are grateful! ! and of course being feature on Pump it up Magazine ;) ! Thanks to our label Winner Zone Entertainment and K Digital Media distribution to make it possible! it is an achievement and we are proud and happy to have them to support our dreams!

7. WHAT'S NEXT FOR YOU? ANY UPCOMING PROJECTS OR TOURS?

We are working on music shows, various contents, and also prepare our second album. Plus the self-composing song of Rumble-G is coming, you can subscribe to our newsletter to get news and updates! Our website is **www.winnerzone.net** and we can follow us on social media:

Instagram: https://instagram.com/rumble_zone/
TikTok: https://vt.tiktok.com/ZSJgTprk6/
Twitter https://twitter.com/RumbleG3/

YOUR MUSIC CONSULTANT

"You Believe And So Do We"

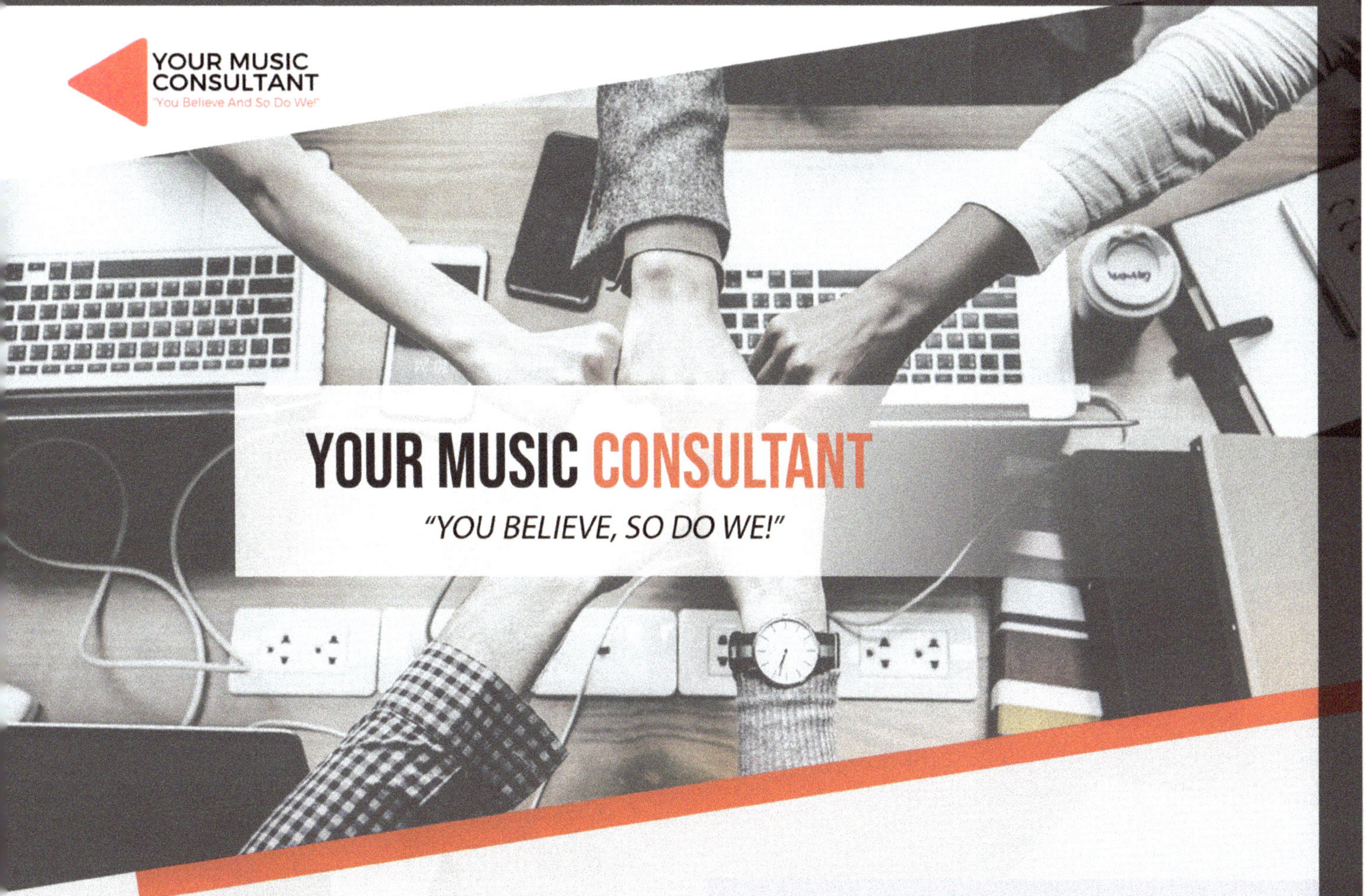

YOUR MUSIC CONSULTANT

"YOU BELIEVE, SO DO WE!"

We Can Help You To Grow Your Business

We are a monthly based service, we put faith in artists who has major potential, believed in them, and who are willing to spend their time and own money to work with us in building a successful music career!

Digital Marketing Services

SOCIAL MEDIA - STREAMING SERVICES - MUSIC DISTRIBUTION - PRESS RELEASE - PRESS DISTRIBUTION - PR

Radio Airplay and TV Commercial

TERRESTRIAL AND DIGITAL RADIO CAMPAIGN AL GENRES EXCEPT HEAVY METAL - CABLE TV AND MAJOR NETWORK COMMERCIAL

Licensing & Booking

CONCERTS, LIVE MUSIC, EVENTS, CLUB NIGHTS - RED CARPETS - FOREIGN LICENSING AND SUBOPUBLISHING

Why Choose Us ?

3 DECADES OF MUSIC BUSINESS EXPERIENCE
Platinium and Gold Records
MOTOWN RECORDS
UNIVERSAL
SONY
CAPITOL RECORDS

WE WORKED WITH:
Kanye West - Jay Z - Stevie Wonder - Michael Jackson - Germaine Jackson Smokey Robinson - Dionne Warwick - Cheryl Lynn - The Originals -

☎ **1 -818-514-0038**
(Ext. 1)
Monday - Friday / 9am to 6pm

LOOKING BACK AT MICHAEL JACKSON'S LIFE!

THE 12TH ANNIVERSARY OF HIS DEATH

It's been 12 years since the world looked down at their phone or TV screens and found out that Michael Jackson passed away at the age of 50. Born August 29, 1958, the singer, songwriter, and dancer known as the "King of Pop" is one of the best-selling artists of all times with an estimated 350 million records worldwide. The 15 time Grammy Award winner left his mark and is one of the most significant cultural figures of the 20th century. From the Jackson 5, Neverland ranch, and more: take a look back at Michael's life and career 12 years after his death.

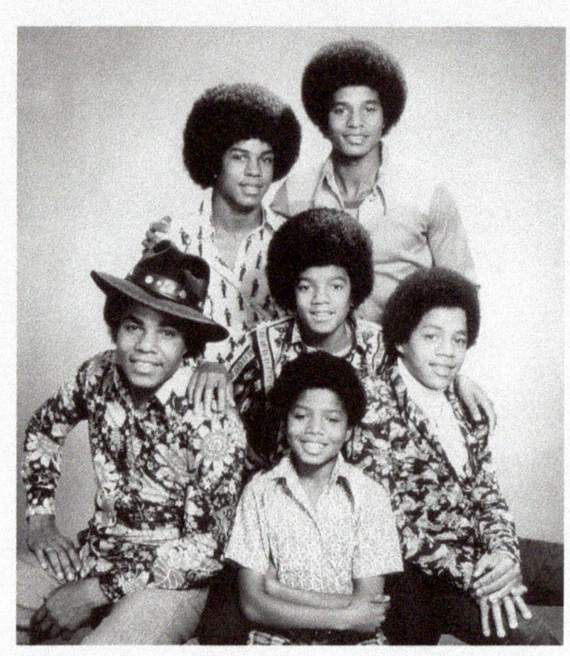

MICHAEL JACKSON CIRCA 1979

He started his solo career in 1971 and became a star with his 1979 album Off the Wall.

His 1982 album Thriller is credited for breaking racial Barries with help of his unforgettable music videos for "Beat It," "Billie Jean," and "Thriller."

The album became the best-selling album of all time.

He went on to release Bad in 1987.

MICHAEL JACKSON 1988

In the late 1980s, people were confused but enthralled by Jackson's changing appearance, behavior, and lifestyle. In 1993 he was accused of sexually abusing the child of a family friend, and it was settled out of civil court due to lack of evidence. From then on, MJ's life was filled with controversy, more allegations, and health problems.

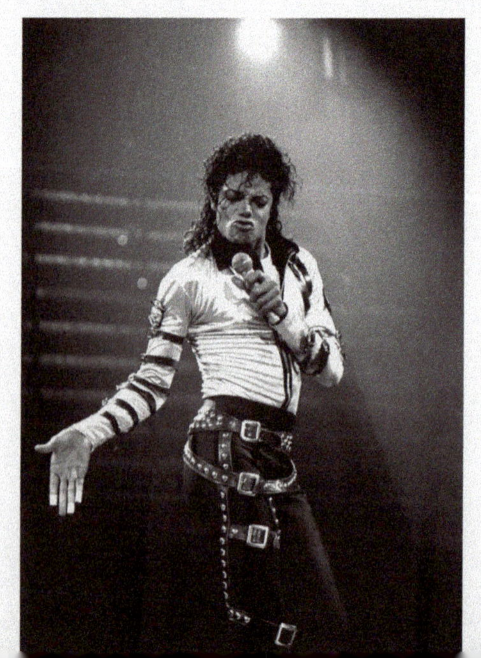

MICHAEL JACKSON AND LISA MARIE PRESLEY AT NEVERLAND RANCH 1995

Jackson purchased an estate that would become Neverland Ranch in 1988. He moved in in 1992 and turned it into his adult childhood fantasy home equipped with a private amusement park, orangutans, and elephants. It was named after the fantasy world in J.M. Barrie's "Peter Pan," about a boy who never grows up. The ranch, of course, has a dark side and he went to trial for allegations of abuse on the property. Following the allegations, he married his first wife Lisa Marie Presley in 1994, they divorced in 1996 and he married Debbie Rowe that year. Rowe gave Birth to their first child Michael Joseph known as "Prince" in February 1997. MJ raised Prince with the help of multiple nannies and nurses. She gave birth to his second child Paris Jackson, in 1998 and they divorced in 1999.

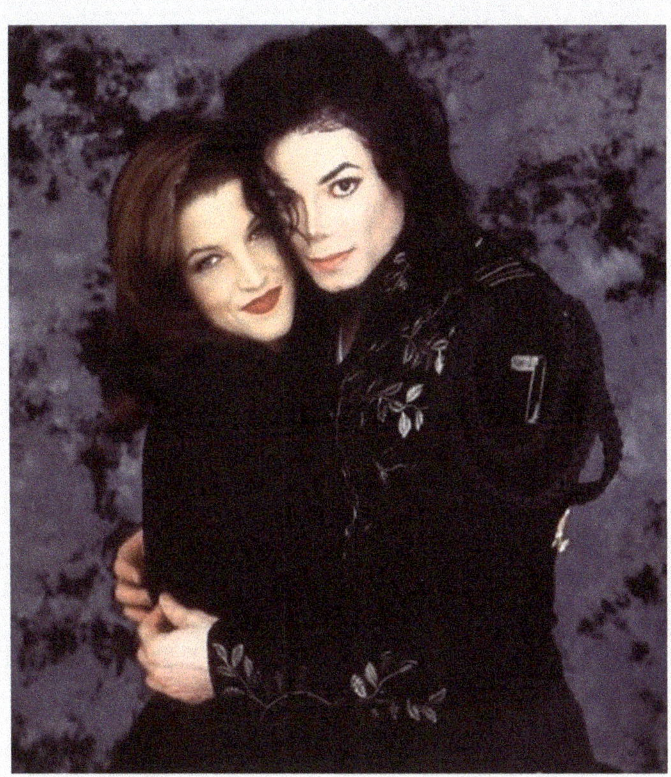

MICHAEL JACKSON, BABY PRINCE MICHAEL II. 2002

During this time MJ made headlines for not only his allegations, but bizarre antics like dangling Prince over a hotel balcony with a blanket over his head in 2002. The world followed his accusations during the People v. Jackson case that went to trial in 2005. If convicted he would have faced up to 2 years in prison. He was acquitted of all charges on June 13th and moved to Bahrain.

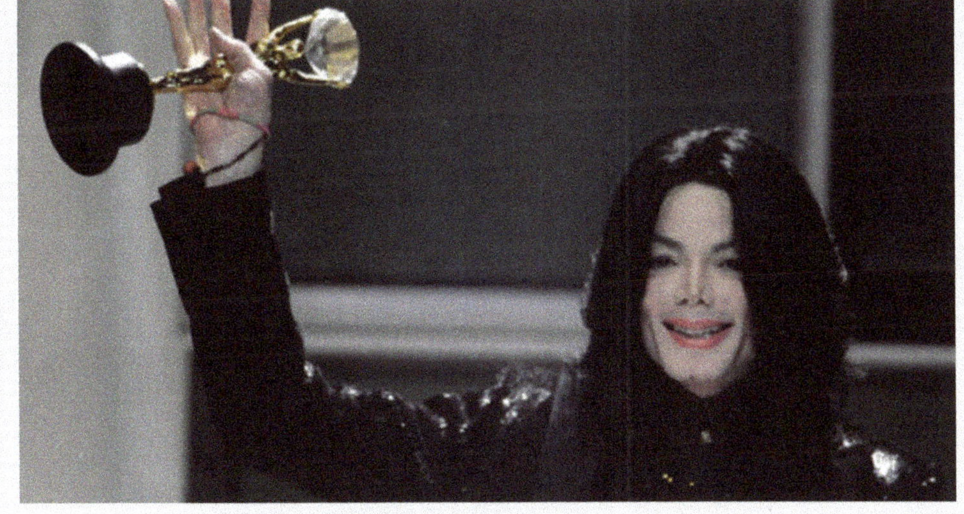

WORLD MUSIC AWARDS 2006

The following year on November 15 2006, Jackson briefly performed "We Are the World" at the World Music Awards in London and accepted the Diamond Award . honoring the sale of over 100 million records, it would be the last performance of his lifetime.

MICHAEL JACKSON 2008

By 2008 MJ was figuring out his finances and debts, transferring Neverland Ranch's title to Sycamore Valley Ranch which earned him $35 million. In 2009 amid speculation of troubles with his health and finances, Michael announced "This Is It," a series of comeback concerts at the 02 arenas, the first since his HIStory World Tour in 1997. The London residency sold over one million tickets in less than two hours and 50 dates were added. MJ moved to Los Angeles to rehearse with director Kenny Ortega, and everything was filmed.

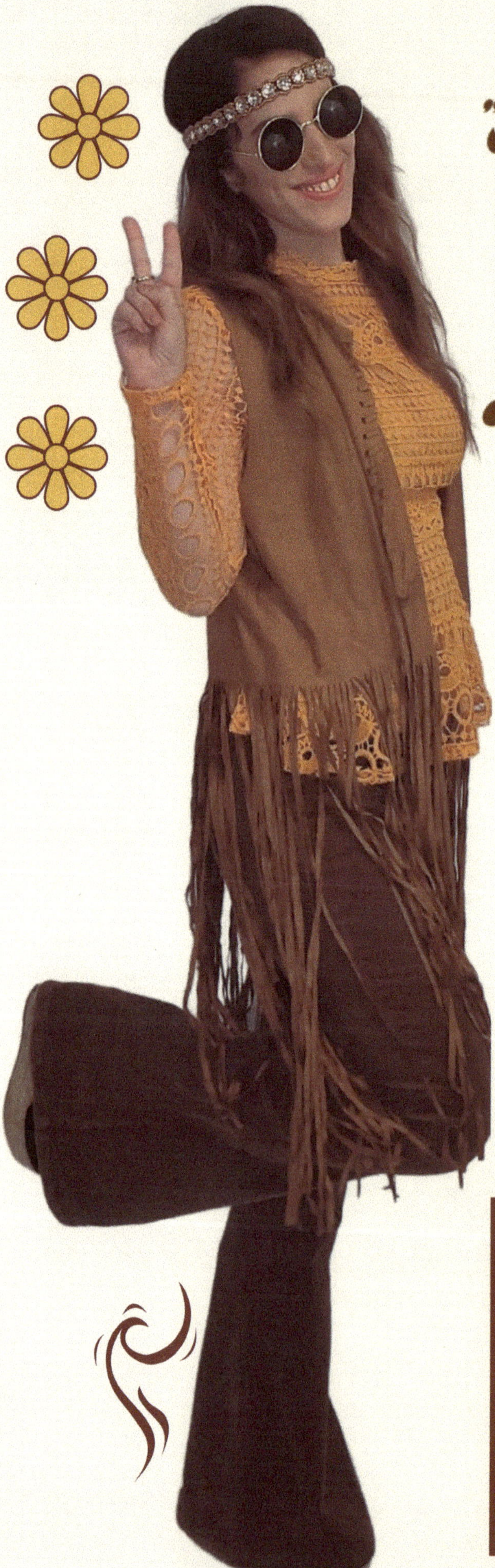

"Dust off your bell bottoms & Let's party like it's 1976!"
Aneessa

Spotify amazon iTunes
TIDAL

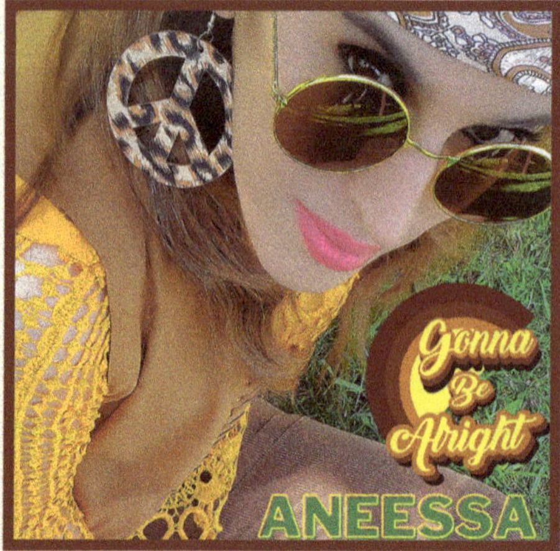

Gonna Be Alright
ANEESSA

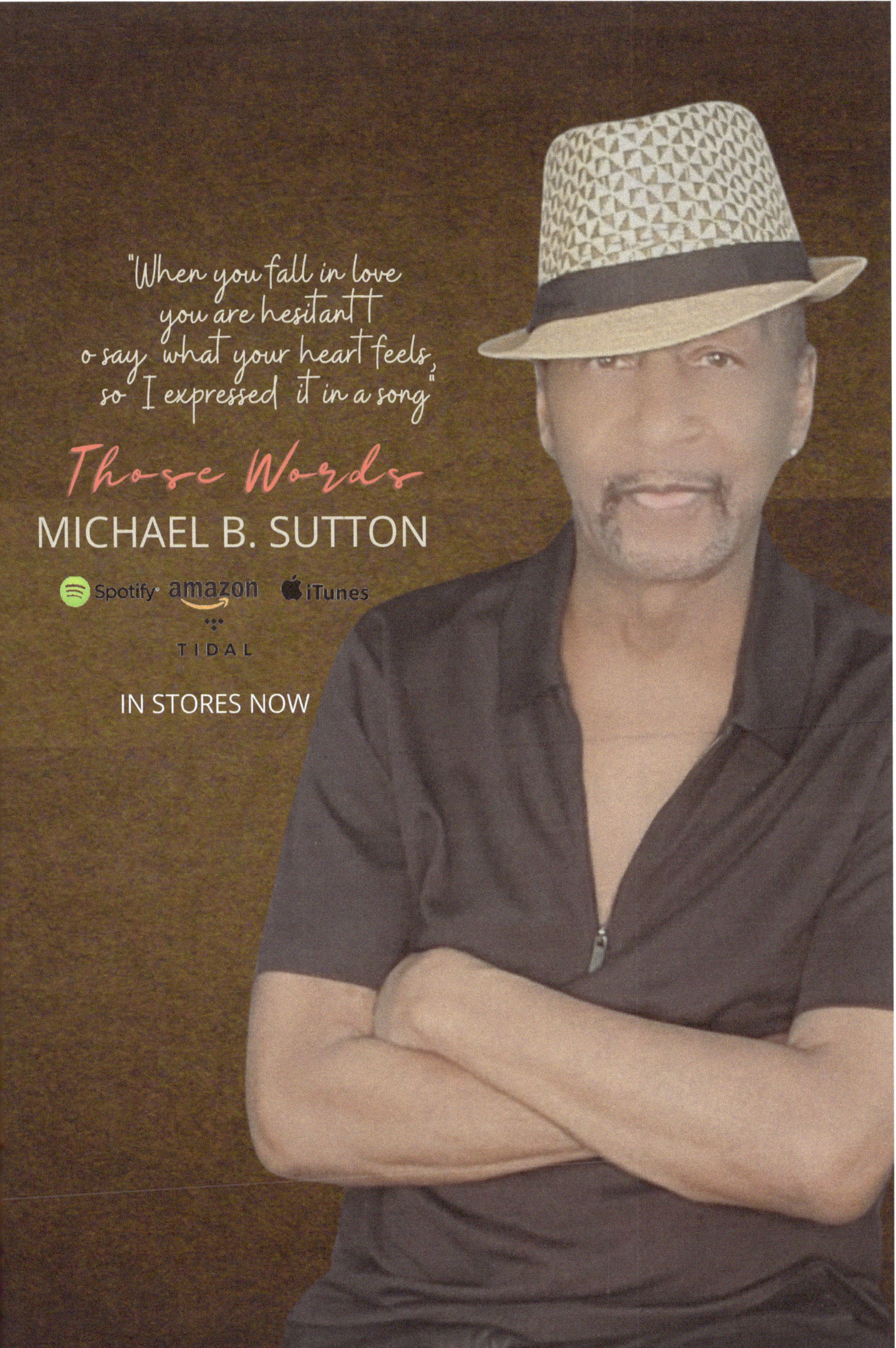
"When you fall in love
you are hesitant t
o say what your heart feels,
so I expressed it in a song"

Those Words

MICHAEL B. SUTTON

Spotify amazon iTunes

TIDAL

IN STORES NOW

Freda Payne

REVIVING THE ICONIC SOUND OF JAZZ MUSIC

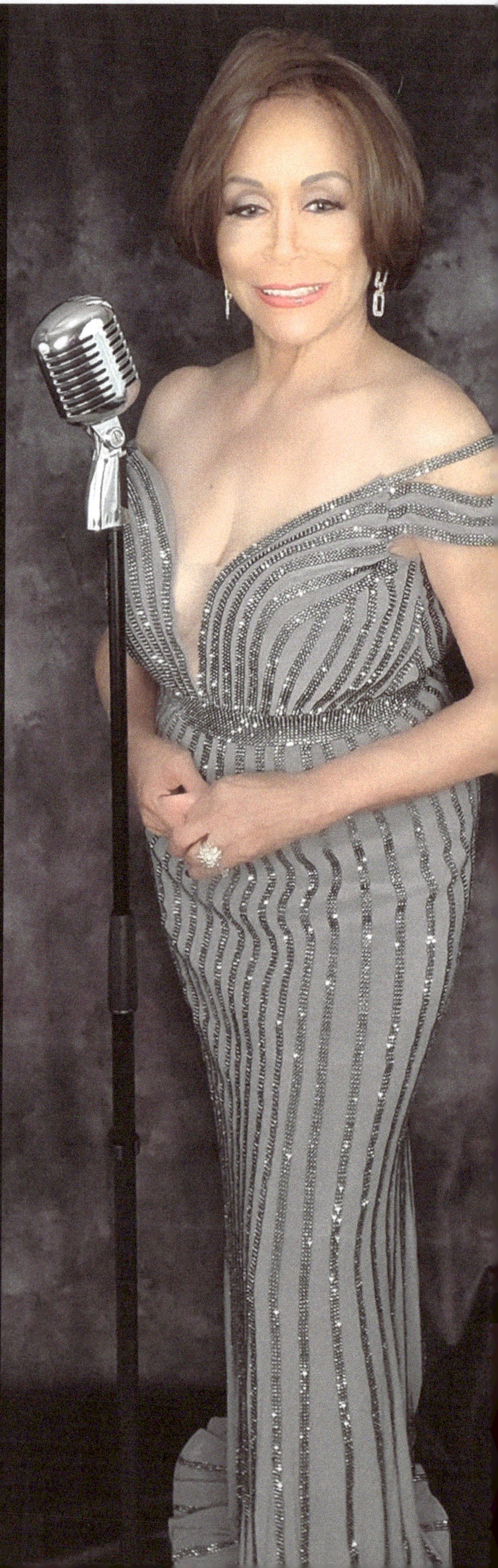

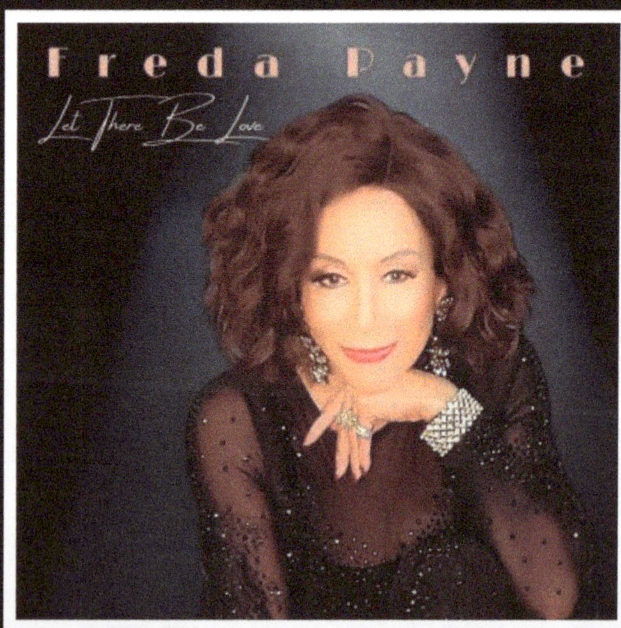

www.FredaPayne.com

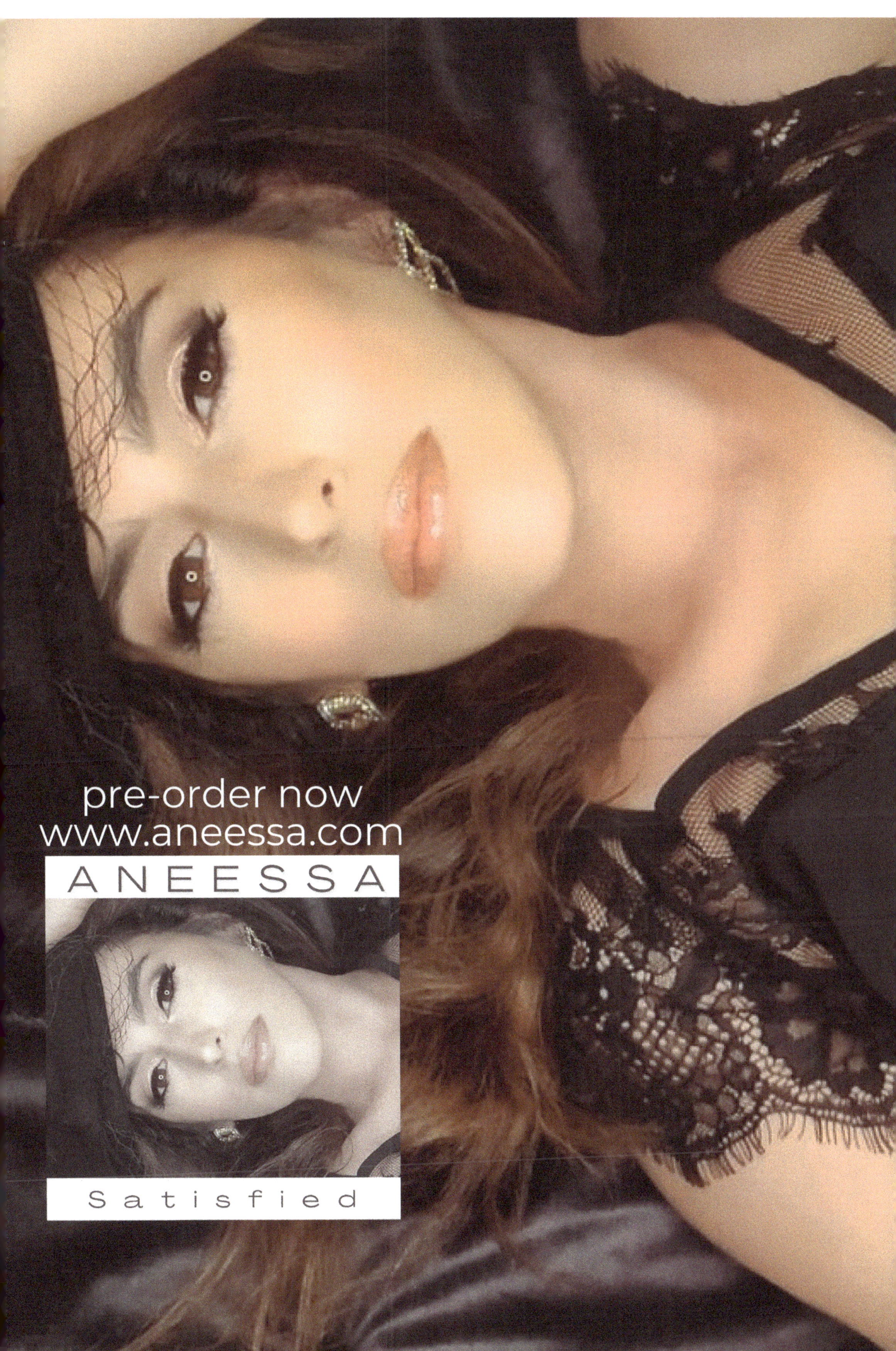

pre-order now
www.aneessa.com
ANEESSA
Satisfied

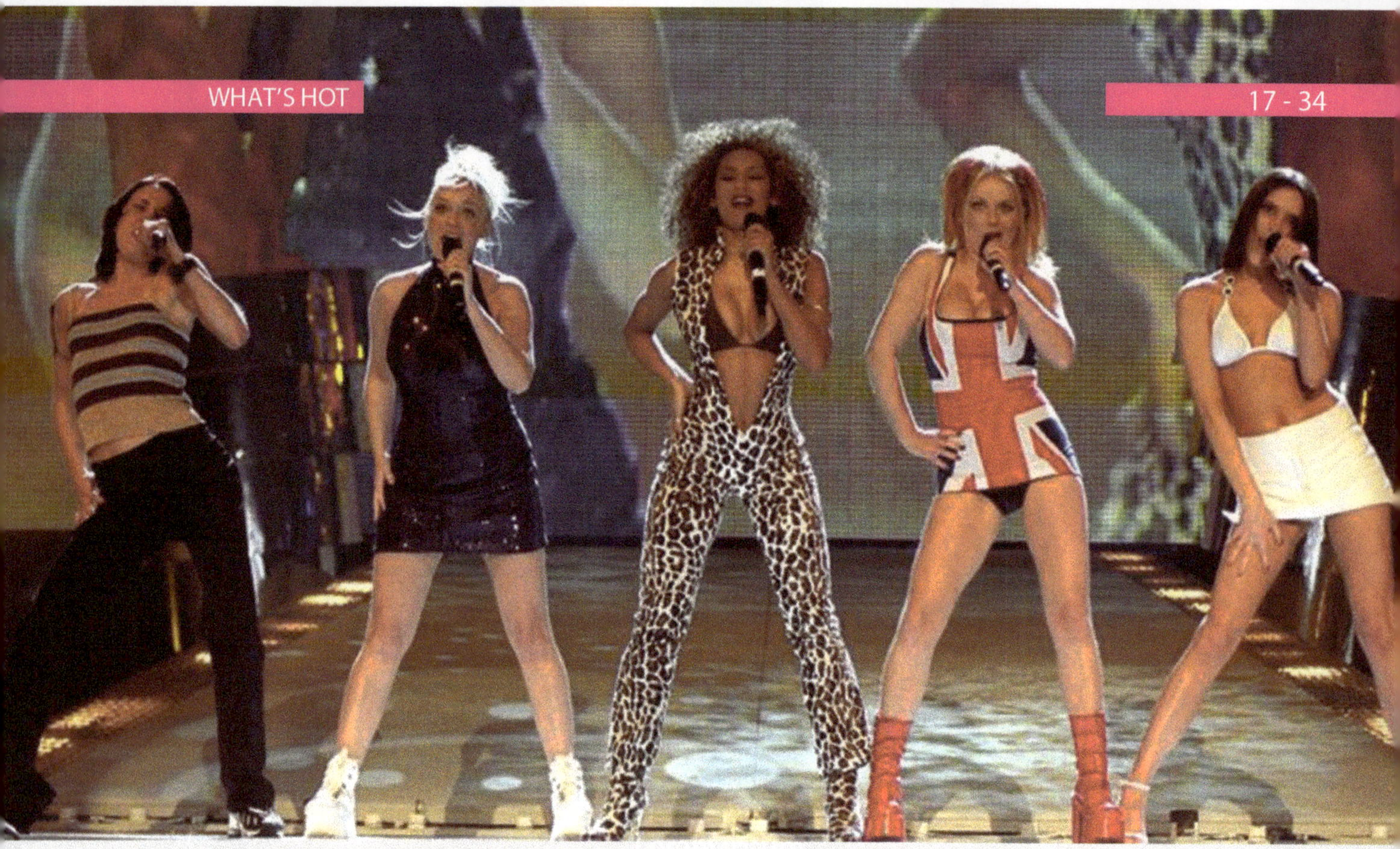

GIRL GROUPS AROUND THE WORLD WE LOVE !

THE SPICE GIRLS ARE THE BEST-SELLING GIRL GROUP IN HISTORY..

When it comes to commercial success, cultural impact and quality of music, the Spice Girls score a solid 10 on each front. 'Wannabe' changed pop music forever, ushering an era of female empowerment never before experienced on such a phenomenal level. The five-piece represented the everyday girl, whether it was through their lyrics of heartache and solidarity, their cheeky sense of fun or generally being bold and brash personalities. And the public absolutely loved it. So much so they went on to sell over 80 million albums during their whirlwind four-year peak.

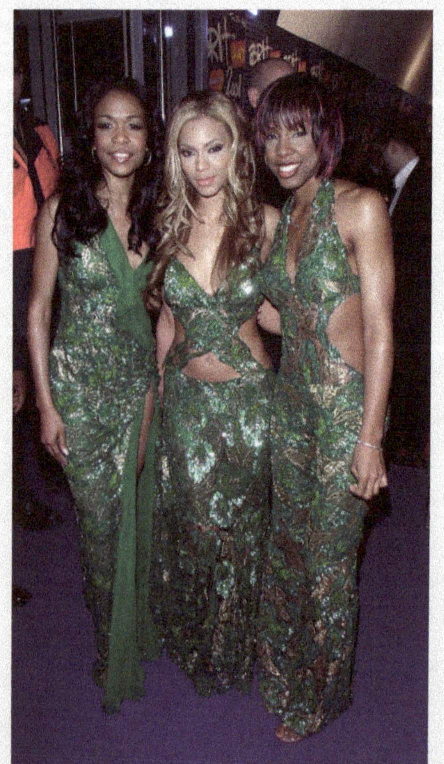

DESTINY'S CHILD GAVE US SIX YEARS OF EMPOWERING ANTHEMS.

Their debut album may have done little to dent the chart despite their first single 'No, No, No' being a hit, but employing the rule of three for a second time gave them the proper breakthrough they needed. 'Bills, Bills, Bills' shot straight to No.1 and The Writing's On The Wall became an instant modern classic. 'Bug a Boo', 'Say My Name' and 'Jumpin' Jumpin'' only cemented their position as the ultimate R&B girl group.

But then came 'Independent Women Part 1', 'Survivor' and 'Bootylicious', and the trio were right: we really couldn't handle this. By the time 'Lose My Breath' and 'Soldier' came along they told us it was Destiny Fulfilled. After selling over 60 million records, they may have had a point.
Their sisterhood is indestructible, so it's not out of the question that they will be on tour soon, , Only Destiny knows the answer right now though.

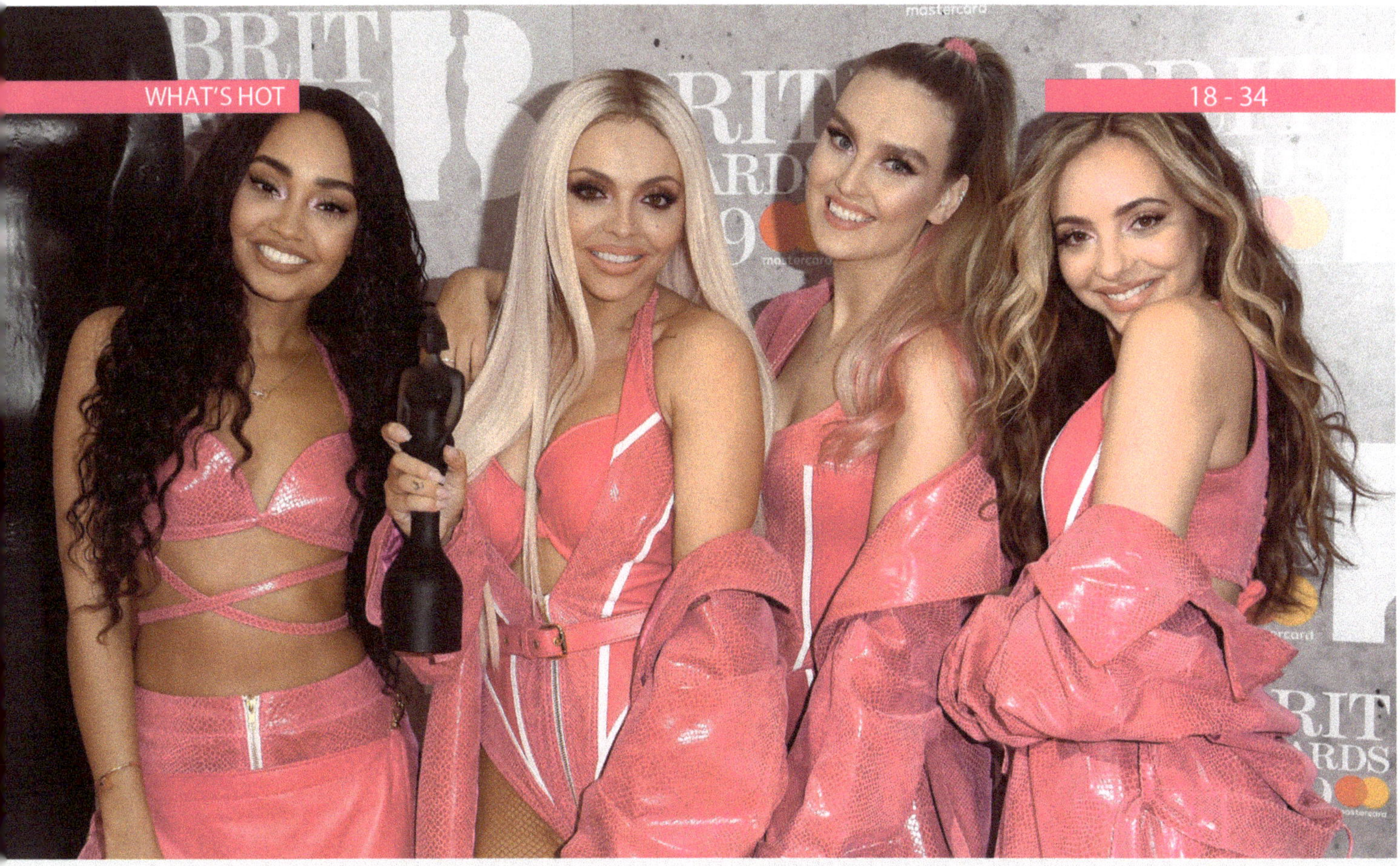

GIRL GROUPS AROUND THE WORLD WE LOVE !

LITTLE MIX HAVE CONTINUED TO DEFY EXPECTATIONS SINCE THEY BECAME THE FIRST EVER GROUP TO WIN THE X FACTOR UK BACK IN 2011.

They've beaten the winner's curse down with loveable pop hits such as 'Wings', 'DNA' and 'Move', and only continued to get even bigger with latest smashes such as 'Black Magic' and 'Hair'.

But while all four of them are extremely talented singers and dancers, it's their warmth and humour that's their main charm. Girl groups have been known to play on tensions within the line-up to provide tabloid column inches, but Little Mix's sisterhood and solidarity has only strengthened their appeal. You don't need negative press when your perfect harmonies and infectious personalities speak loud enough for themselves.

IT'S TAKEN JUST FOUR YEARS FOR BLACKPINK TO BECOME ONE OF THE BIGGEST GIRL GROUP IN THE WORLD!

They were the first K-pop girl group to play at Coachella and to reach 1bn YouTube views — now they're the most-subscribed-to music group on the platform — as well as being the first girl group from any country to feature on Forbes Asia's 30 Under 30 list.

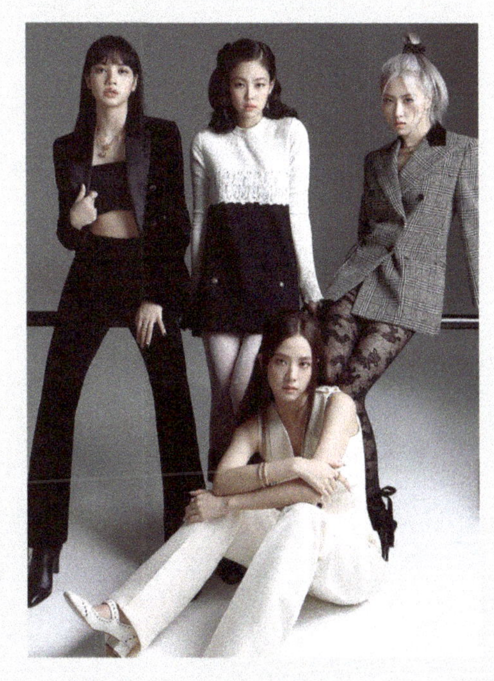

In 2019, they broke three Guinness World Records with the single Kill This Love, which has had more than 312m plays on Spotify and over 824m YouTube views — a mere fraction of the quartet's billions of streams, downloads, views and followers. That same year they also undertook the most financially successful concert tour by a Korean female group. They're front-row fixtures at runway shows and the faces of mega brands including Chanel, Puma, Louis Vuitton and Dior. And all this with just a handful of songs in their repertoire.

NICOLETTE SULLIVAN

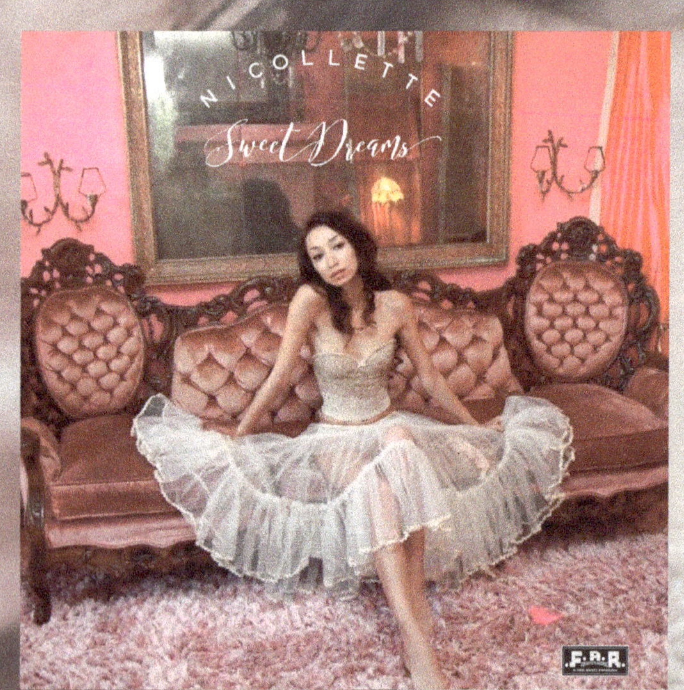

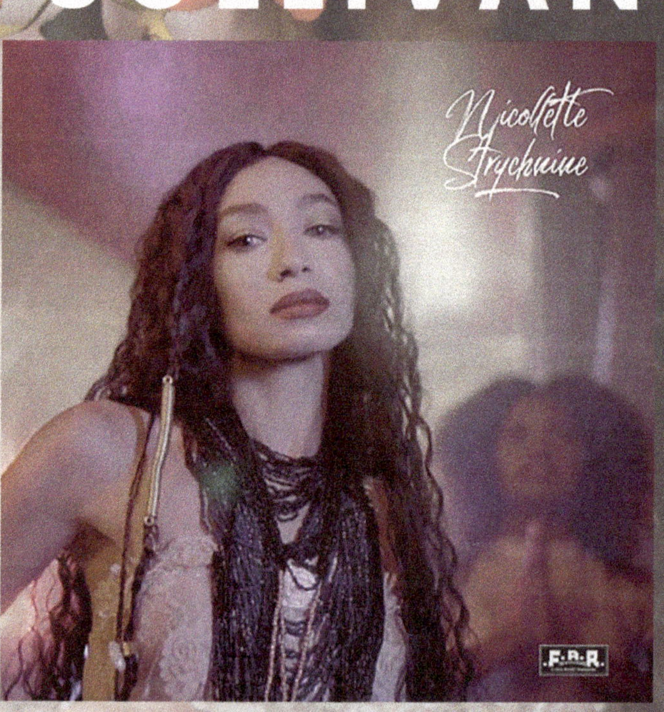

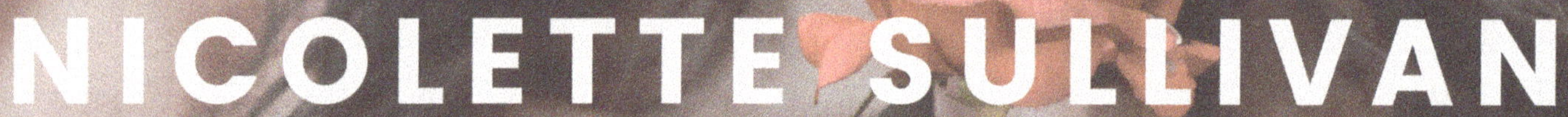

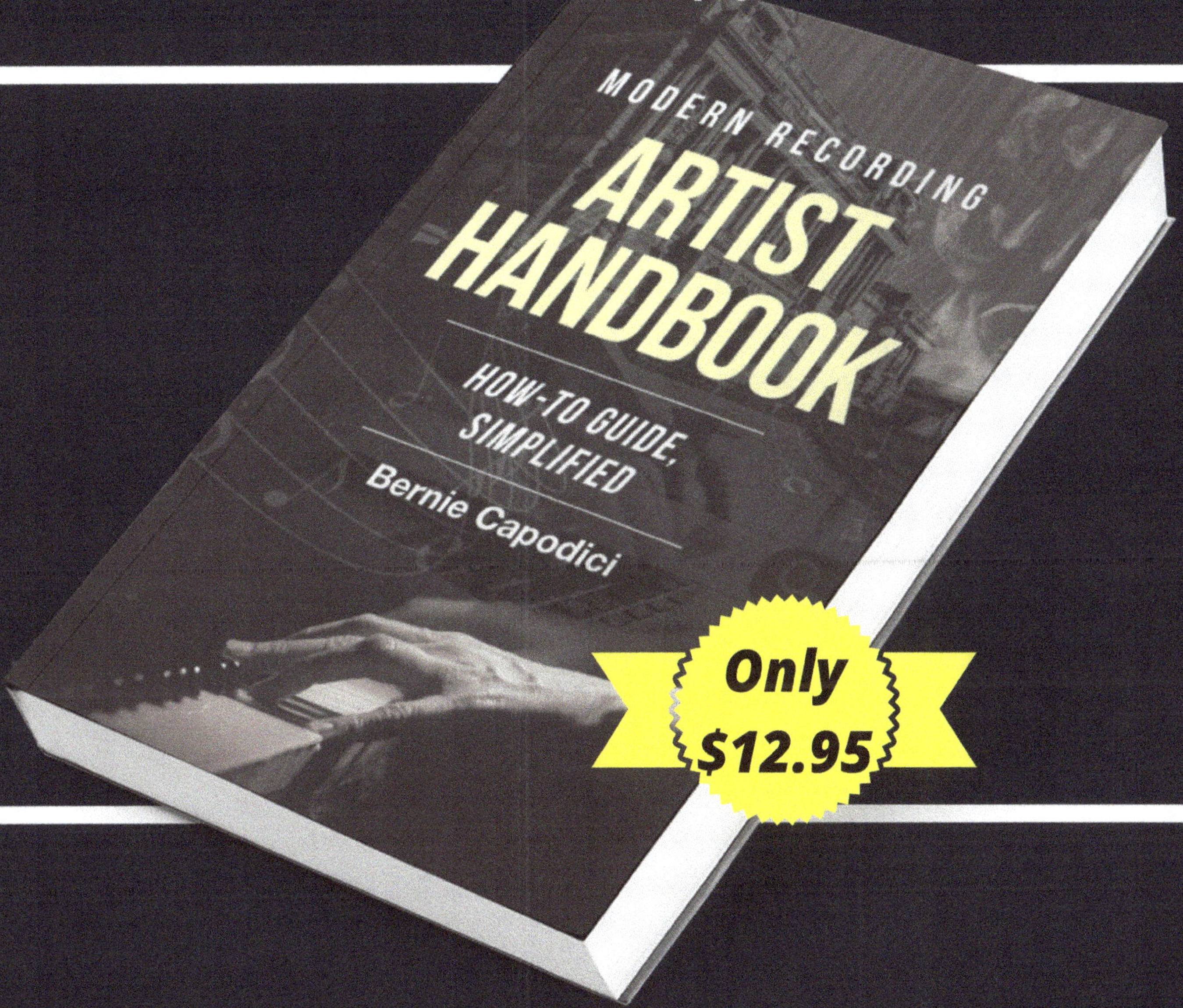

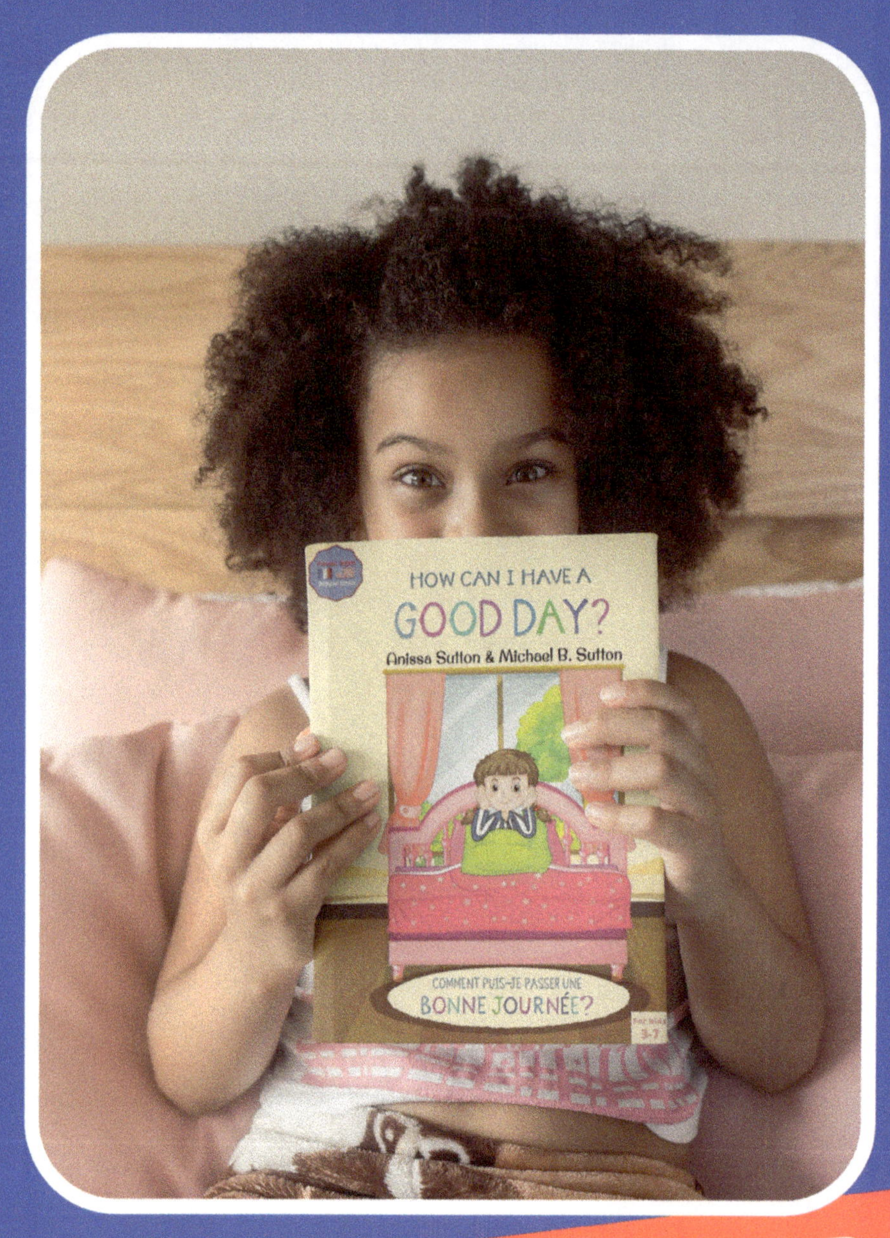

How Can I Have A Good Day?
Comment Puis-Je Passer Une Bonne Journée?

FRENCH - ENGLISH

ENCOURAGE YOUR CHILD TO LEARN FRENCH & APPRECIATE THE FAMILY AND PEOPLE AROUND THEM

WWW.EDITIONS-LA.COM

MUST READ FOR WOMEN IN THE MUSIC INDUSTRY

1. ALL YOU NEED TO KNOW ABOUT THE MUSIC BUSINESS (10TH EDITION)

Referred to by the Los Angeles Times as "the industry bible," this book deserves a spot at the top of everyone's music business reading list.

It's written by Donald S. Passman, an entertainment lawyer who works with some of the biggest names and companies in the business. So, he knows what he's talking about when it comes to the music industry

Having been around for over 25 years, with updates made to it on a regular basis, the latest edition is one of the most relevant guides on the subject. Whether you're a songwriter, manager, promoter, lawyer or any other music business professional, you'll find something in this book for you.

2. REAL ARTISTS DON'T STARVE

This is a must read book for anybody chasing a career in the music business. It challenges the stigma of the "starving artist" and aims to give readers the proper mindset for success in music.

It teaches the importance of strategic risks, how making money can help your art, why collaboration is integral to success and lots more.

It's a realistic and refreshing point of view on an industry that can be overly pessimistic when it comes to making a living

3. YOUR BAND IS A VIRUS – EXPANDED EDITION (VOLUME 2)

Without proper marketing and song promotion, even the best music will fall flat. This is why it's important that independent artists learn how to effectively grow their listener base and get their music out into the world.

In this book, you'll discover the secrets to a powerful release, how to approach bloggers and writers, building upon past achievements and more.

Even applying just a few of the tactics that are explained will have a tremendous effect on how your music is received by the industry.

Even applying just a few of the tactics that are explained will have a tremendous effect on how your music is received by the industry.

4. MUSIC LAW SERIES (VOLUME 1 & VOLUME 2)

If you've been looking for a book that covers all the legal ins and outs of a successful career in the music business, look no further.

This massive work spans two books and was written by one of the industry's leading entertainment lawyers.

In it you'll discover advice on everything from earning royalties, owning masters, sampling music, negotiating contracts, managing debt, how to avoid being sued, trademarks vs copyright, filing taxes and so much more.

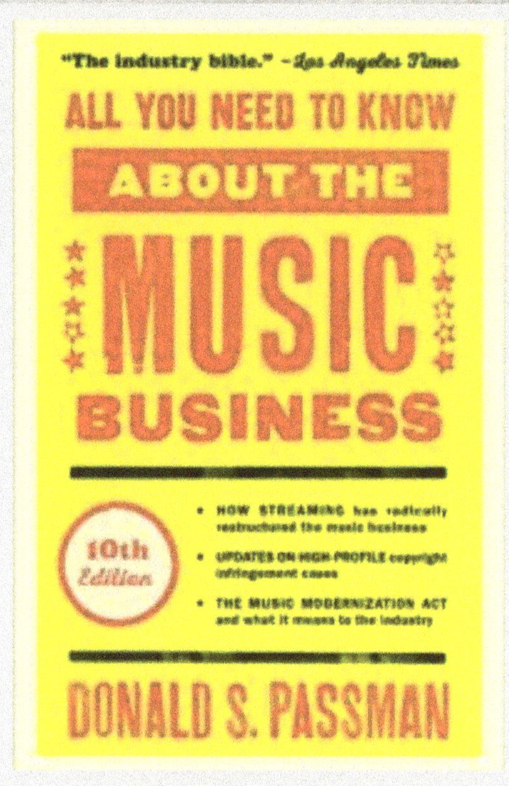
"The industry bible." - Los Angeles Times
ALL YOU NEED TO KNOW
ABOUT THE
MUSIC
BUSINESS
10th Edition
• HOW STREAMING has radically restructured the music business
• UPDATES ON HIGH-PROFILE copyright infringement cases
• THE MUSIC MODERNIZATION ACT and what it means to the industry
DONALD S. PASSMAN

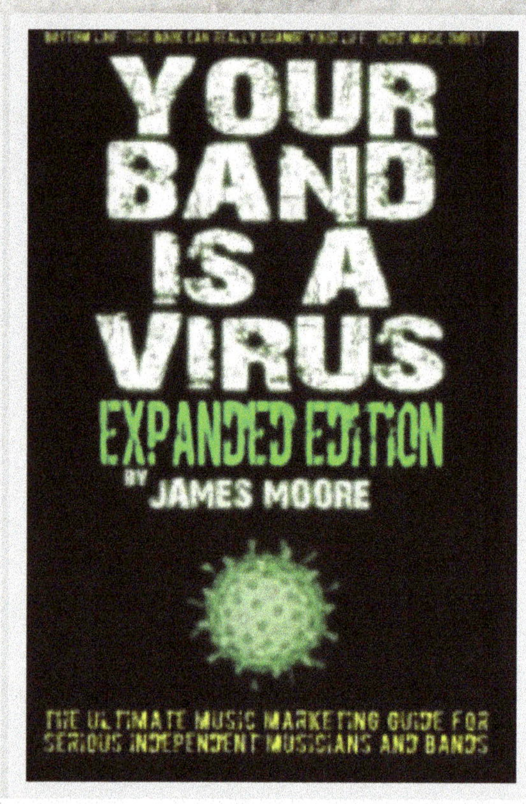
YOUR
BAND
IS A
VIRUS
EXPANDED EDITION
BY JAMES MOORE
THE ULTIMATE MUSIC MARKETING GUIDE FOR
SERIOUS INDEPENDENT MUSICIANS AND BANDS

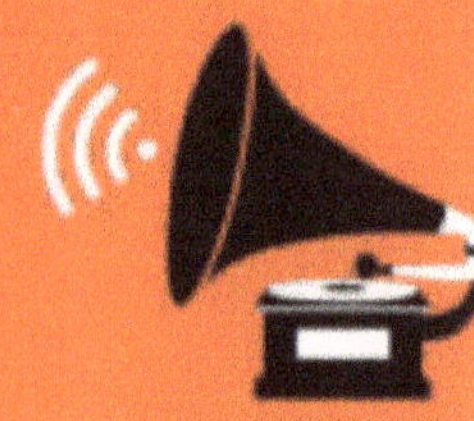
SECOND EDITION
How to Make
It in the
New Music
Business
Practical Tips on Building
a Loyal Following and
Making a Living as a Musician
Ari Herstand

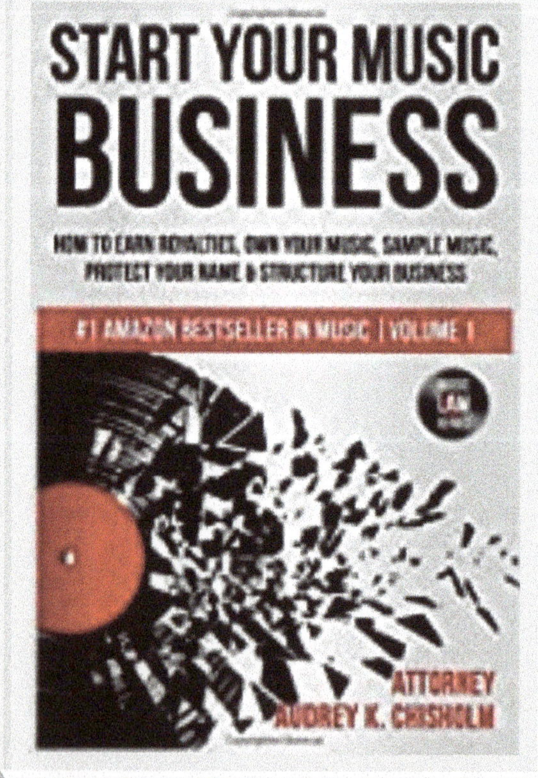
START YOUR MUSIC
BUSINESS
HOW TO EARN ROYALTIES, OWN YOUR MUSIC, SAMPLE MUSIC,
PROTECT YOUR NAME & STRUCTURE YOUR BUSINESS
#1 AMAZON BESTSELLER IN MUSIC | VOLUME 1
ATTORNEY
AUDREY K. CHISHOLM

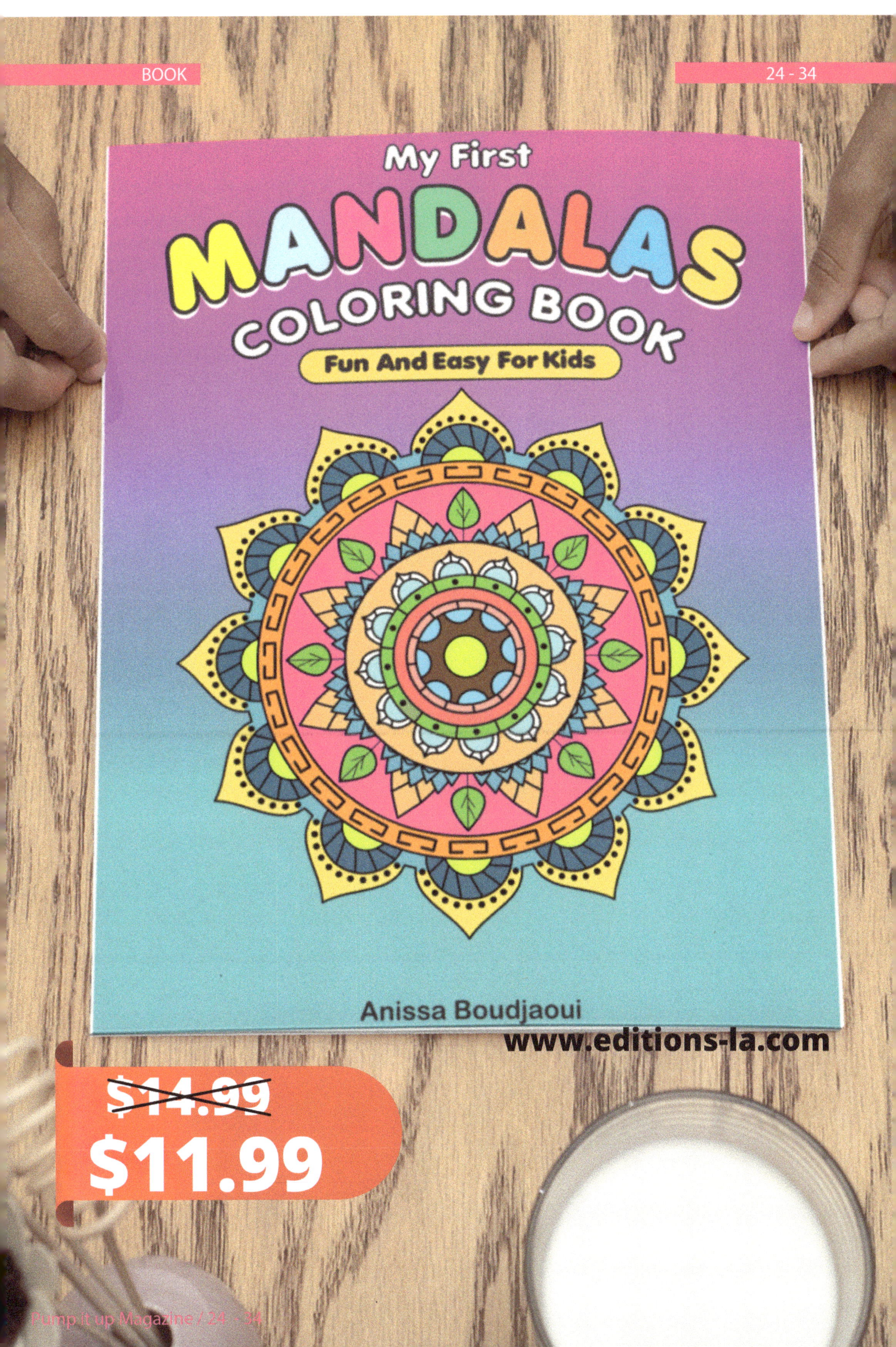
My First
MANDALAS
COLORING BOOK
Fun And Easy For Kids
Anissa Boudjaoui
www.editions-la.com
$14.99
$11.99

HOW TO CHOOSE THE RIGHT SUNSCREEN

After all these freezing months, finally summer is coming. Summer officially begins in June but since it's now spring, and the weather has become warmer. We already talk to you about the korean skincare transition from winter to summer but you maybe need to learn more about one step. As I'm sure most of you know, now that the sun's out more often, and you should wear sunscreen everyday. In fact, you should always wear sunscreen no matter the weather as it protects your skin from sunspots, aging, wrinkles, and potentially skin cancer. But do you know everything you need to know about it?

HOW TO CHOOSE YOUR SUNSCREEN

#1 The SPF of your sunscreen, whether it's for your face only or the rest of your body, should always be higher than 30 SPF. SPF refers to "sun protection factor", which is a measure of how a sunscreen will protect you from UV (ultraviolet) B rays, which cause the most reddening and damage to the skin. One of the most important part of sunscreen, though, is reapplying it ever 1-2 hours (regardless of the SPF), specially if you are outside.

#2 Avoid the sprayed type of sunscreens as the layer you will apply might be too thin and will make it even less effective. You should apply a thick, even layer

#3 There's actually no waterproof sunscreen, only water resistant ones. The only way to get maximum coverage is to reapply it.

HOW TO USE YOUR SUNSCREEN

#4 Your sunscreen should be applied at the end of your skincare routine, after your moisturizer and before you put on your makeup. It's preferable if it's applied around 20 minutes before going out, whether you decide to wear makeup or not.

#5 If you sweat a lot, go swimming or are outside / exposed to the sun for multiple hours, you should make sure to reapply it often, preferably the recommended every 1-2 hours. Please, don't use expired sunscreen as it would not be efficient, or it could even cause some allergic reaction.

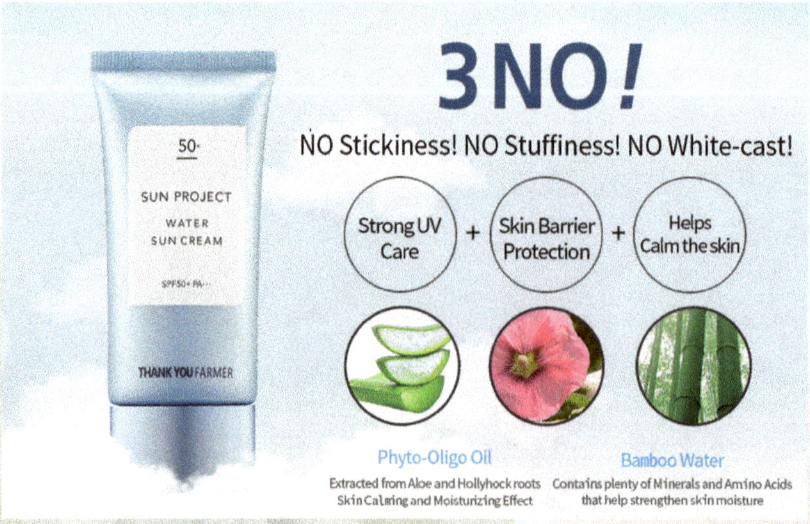

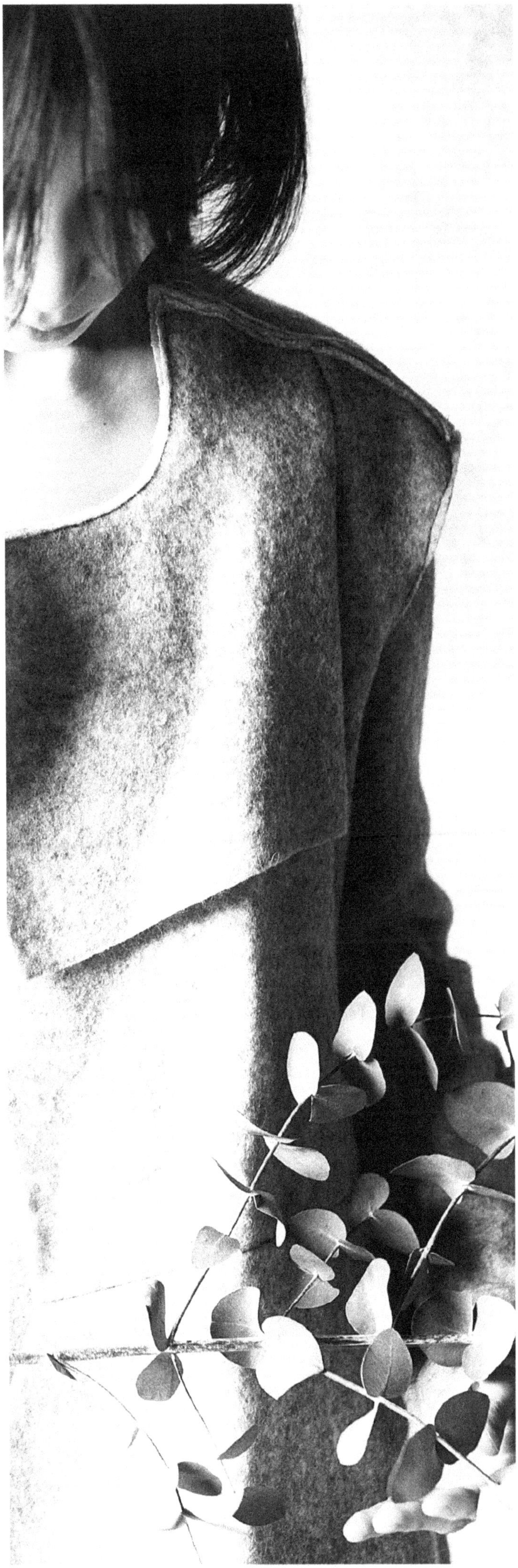

SUMMER TRENDS MUST HAVE
EVERYTHING YOU NEED TO KNOW

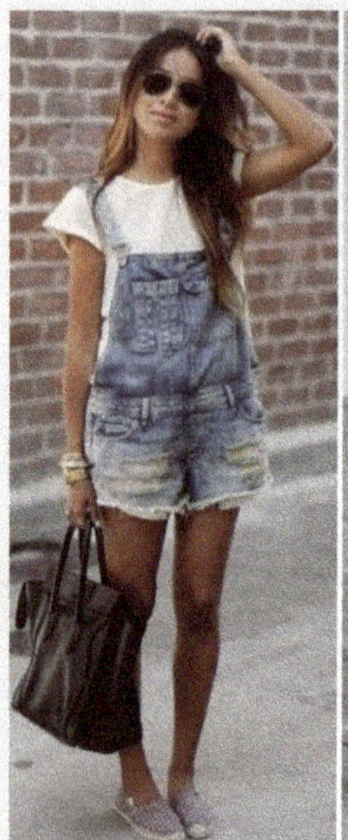 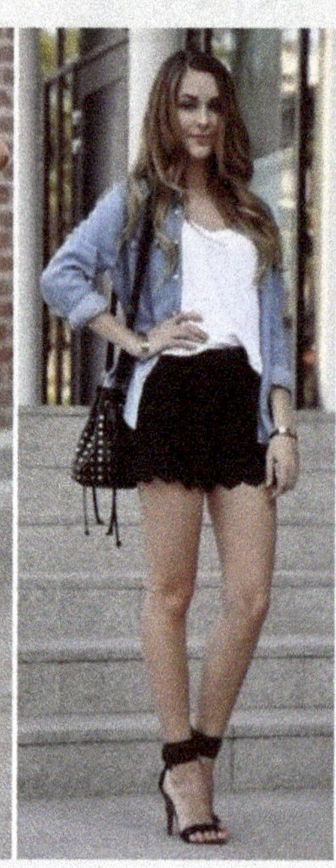 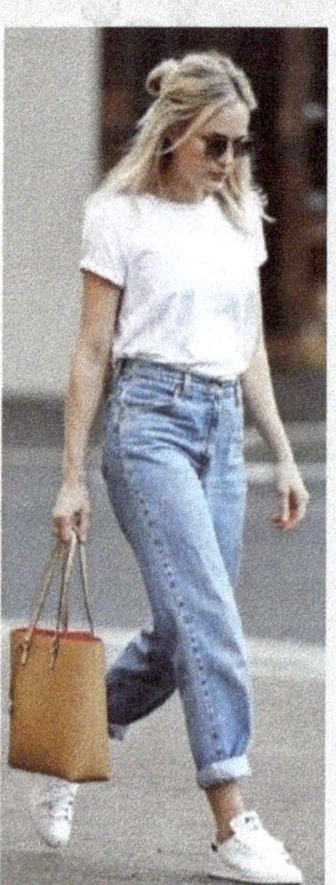 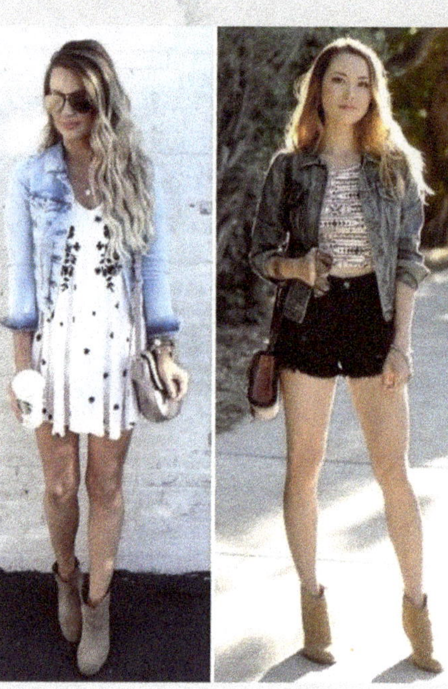 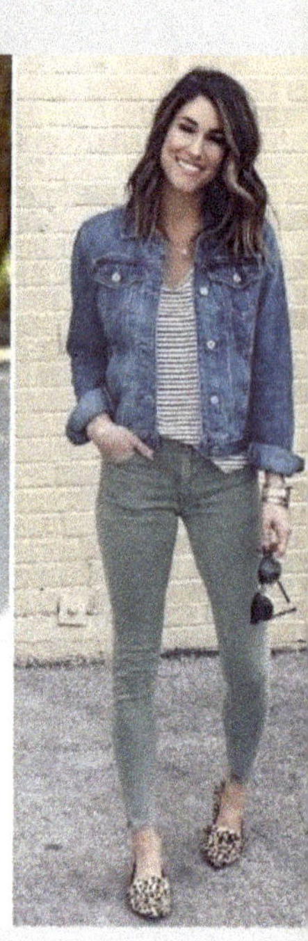

DENIM JACKET

Denim jackets come in many different styles and cuts, allowing you to find the perfect complement to your summer wardrobe. Practical for layering on a chilly morning or breezy night, the jean jacket is a closet staple that looks cool and stylish as the finishing touch for any outfit. Comfortable and versatile, you can pair your denim jacket with all kinds of pants and shirts to design a vibe that fits your fashion and personality.

SKINNY JEANS

In recent years, skinny jeans have transitioned from fashion trend to classic closet staple. Great for casual and business casual looks, you can't go wrong with a pair of fitted skinny jeans. Just add your favorite t-shirt, tank top, or blouse to match the weather and dress code. Skinny jeans also pair well with different shoe options, so play around to find your desired style.

ANKLE STRAP HEELS

Ankle-strap heels are classic summer footwear for a reason. From heeled sandals to two-strap heels, these shoe styles offer a great way to dress up for summer celebrations without having to wear uncomfortable pumps. Grab a pair of neutral wedges for the day and check out block heel sandals for a night out with friends.

WHITE SHIRTS

When buying summer basics, you'll want to get white shirts in several styles and designs. White will reflect the sun and keep you cool in the heat while complementing your tan and lighter hair from days spent at the beach. From the breezy button-down to a sleeveless top, a white shirt can match any outfit, so try the style with your favorite jeans, skirts, and dresses to create your desired looks.

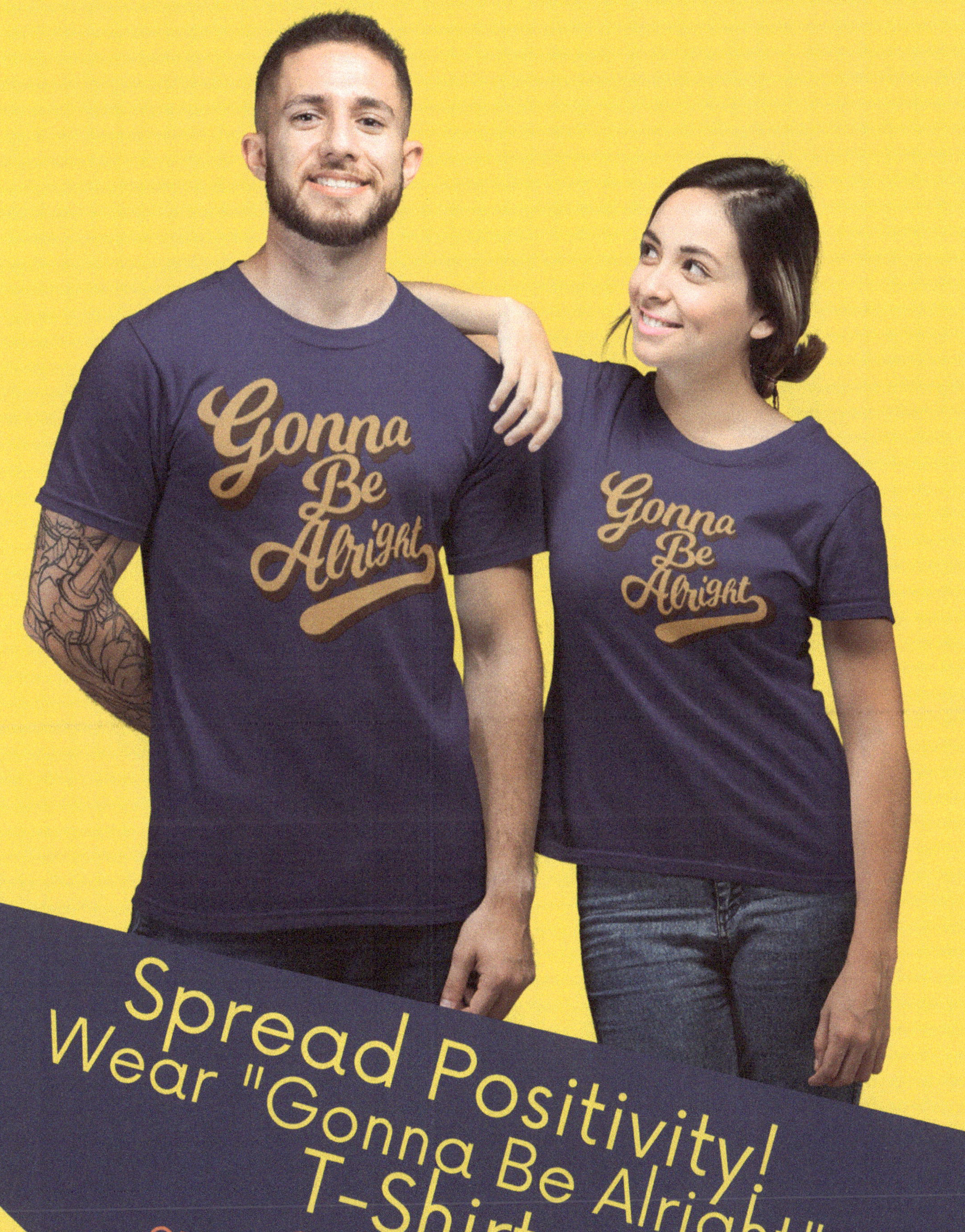
Spread Positivity!
Wear "Gonna Be Alright"
T-Shirt
ORDER NOW
ON ANEESSA MERCH STORE
WWW.ANEESSA.COM

HOW TO FIND
AN AUDIENCE
FOR YOUR MUSIC

1. GET CLEAR ON WHO YOU ARE

Before you even think about strategizing how to find your target audience, you want to make sure you're crystal clear on who you are and the message you want to convey.

Think about your favorite well-known artist and tell me what comes to mind. I doubt you're fumbling around trying to put the pieces together and that's because they have a really solid brand.

For instance: What do you think of when you think of Halsey? Mental health. LGBTQ rights. Social justice.

What about Taylor Swift? Her brand may seem to change with nearly every album cycle but there are serious consistencies that mean you and I always strike up some very clear imagery when we think of her. She takes risks. Offers her fans connection. Empowerment. And love her or hate her, she's a force to be reckoned with.

Think about your favorite bands and see what comes to mind instantly. Your fans should be able to do the same when it comes to you. Because in order to find your target audience and know who they are and what they feel, believe, and desire, you need to first know who it is you are.

2. TAKE NOTE OF WHAT OTHER BANDS ARE DOING

Find a couple of artists who are in the position you want to be, in a similar genre, and make a serious case study out of them to figure out what they've done to get there and what they continue to do to stay there.

Find artists who are in the position you want to be in, say, another two or three years. It's not realistic to compare yourself to a major label artist because they're operating with an existing fanbase that quite frankly isn't going anywhere even if they fail to post to social media or take another three years to put out an album.

So find artists who are more established than you are, but still growing (i.e. not necessarily signed to a label or touring the world, but who are playing more of the kind of shows you want, getting the endorsements your after, the Spotify playlists you want, etc.) then you'll have a really good idea of what's working.

Study what they do and how they do it. How do they interact with their audience? What platforms are they on? What kind of venues do they play? What kind of merch do they have? What cities are they popular in? What hashtags are they using to get in front of their fans? (tip: make a Google Doc of different groups of hashtags to use, so when it's time to post to IG you can simply copy and paste your go-to hashtags. Having a few different groups to choose from means mixing it up so that IG will favor you in the algorithm. For whatever reason, if you use the same 10 hashtags over and over, IG tends not to like that. Probably because they think you're a robot.).

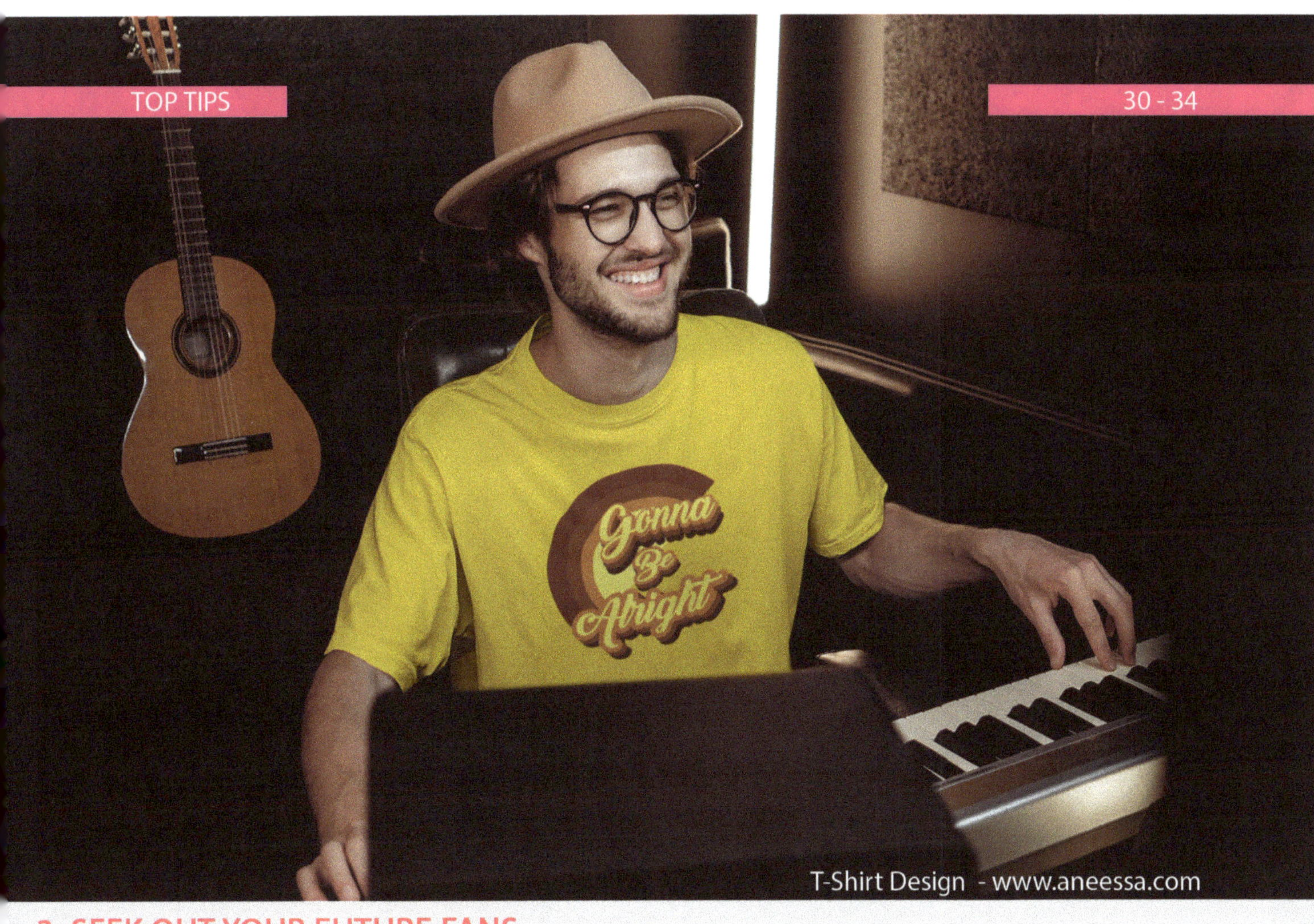

T-Shirt Design - www.aneessa.com

3. SEEK OUT YOUR FUTURE FANS

There are a lot of ways to find new fans. Offline, shows are a great place to get in front of new faces. This can be at your own shows or (and especially) the shows of others. Sometimes this means going to other artist's shows and interacting with the audience, maybe hanging at the merch booth if one of the artists on the bill is your friend, and just getting to know people and introducing yourself. It can also mean standing outside venues of major label artist's shows and getting to know everyone in line, having a conversation, and eventually sharing your music and asking if they want to sign up to your mailing list on the spot.

Online it can mean joining different Facebook groups and getting involved by offering feedback on fellow artist's posts, commenting with your own stories and thoughts, and just getting involved in your online communities.

On Instagram it can mean finding artists that have a similar sound and are of a similar size to you and seeing who their fans are. If those fans they seem like they might like your music, then get to know them by following and commenting on their posts.

At the end of the day, building a community isn't only one of the smartest things you can do for your career, it's honestly one of the most fulfilling. Because when you get down to it, we got into this to build a connection.

And sure, it can be overwhelming sometimes to keep up with all the day-to-day. But don't forget why you got into this—to make a difference. To meet others who are just like you. To tell your story and hope it connects with someone else.

So find artists who are more established than you are, but still growing (i.e. not necessarily signed to a label or touring the world, but who are playing more of the kind of shows you want, getting the endorsements your after, the Spotify playlists you want, etc.) then you'll have a really good idea of what's working.

tags over and over, IG tends not to like that. Probably because they think you're a robot.).

OFFICIAL SELECTION 2021
sundance
film festival

RITA MORENO
JUST A GIRL WHO DECIDED TO GO FOR IT

STARRING
RITA MORENO & FRIENDS

EVA LONGORIA   GEORGE CHAKIRIS   GLORIA ESTEFAN   HÉCTOR ELIZONDO
KAREN OLIVO   JUSTINA MACHADO   LIN-MANUEL MIRANDA   MITZI GAYNOR
MORGAN FREEMAN   NORMAN LEAR   TERRENCE MCNALLY   WHOOPI GOLDBERG

AMERICAN MASTERS PICTURES AND ACT III PRODUCTIONS IN ASSOCIATION WITH ARTEMIS RISING AND MARAMARA FILMS
PRESENT RITA MORENO JUST A GIRL WHO DECIDED TO GO FOR IT
MUSIC BY KATHRYN BOSTIC EDITORS KEVIN KLAUBER, ACE & MARIEM PÉREZ RIERA DIRECTOR OF PHOTOGRAPHY PJ LÓPEZ, SPC
SUPERVISING PRODUCER FOR AMERICAN MASTERS JUNKO TSUNASHIMA AMERICAN MASTERS SERIES PRODUCER JULIE SACKS
EXECUTIVE PRODUCERS MICHAEL KANTOR   REGINA SCULLY   NORMAN LEAR   LIN-MANUEL MIRANDA
CO PRODUCED BY ILIA J. VÉLEZ-DÁVILA PRODUCED BY BRENT MILLER, p.g.a.
PRODUCED AND DIRECTED BY MARIEM PÉREZ RIERA

AMERICAN MASTERS PICTURES
PBS

WORLD HUMANITARIAN DAY
AUGUST 19

#TheHumanRace

A global challenge for climate action in solidarity with the people who need it most The climate emergency is wreaking havoc across the world at a scale that people on the front lines and in the humanitarian community cannot manage. Time is already running out for the world's most vulnerable people — those who have contributed least to the global climate emergency yet are hit the hardest — and millions of others that are already losing their homes, their livelihoods, and their lives.

Providing life-saving support during the pandemic

On World Humanitarian Day (WHD) August 19, the world commemorates humanitarian workers killed and injured in the course of their work, and we honour all aid and health workers who continue, despite the odds, to provide life-saving support and protection to people most in need.

This year World Humanitarian Day comes as the world continues to fight the COVID-19 pandemic over recent months.

Aid workers are overcoming unprecedented access hurdles to assist people in humanitarian crises in 54 countries, as well as in a further nine countries which have been catapulted into humanitarian need by the COVID-19 pandemic.

This day was designated in memory of the 19 August 2003 bomb attack on the Canal Hotel in Baghdad, Iraq, killing 22 people, including the chief humanitarian in Iraq, Sergio Vieira de Mello. In 2009, the United Nations General Assembly formalized the day as World Humanitarian Day.

Support our #RealLifeHeroes this World Humanitarian Day

It is true that our obsession with myths and legends has been with us since the dawn of culture. Their fictional fantastic feats, embodied enemies, and arduous journeys teach us how to dream big and summon the courage needed to do what's right.

However, the heroes of our world, here and now, are just as worthy of admiration and celebration because they're real — they're real: choosing to help in the most extreme circumstances — and their stories show that real life heroes exhibit an uncanny ability to persevere despite the odds, and to do so with humility and dedication.

Stand in solidarity with the world's most vulnerable people by using these hashtags in your social media activities
#TheHumanRace #WorldHumanitarianDay #RealLifeHeroes

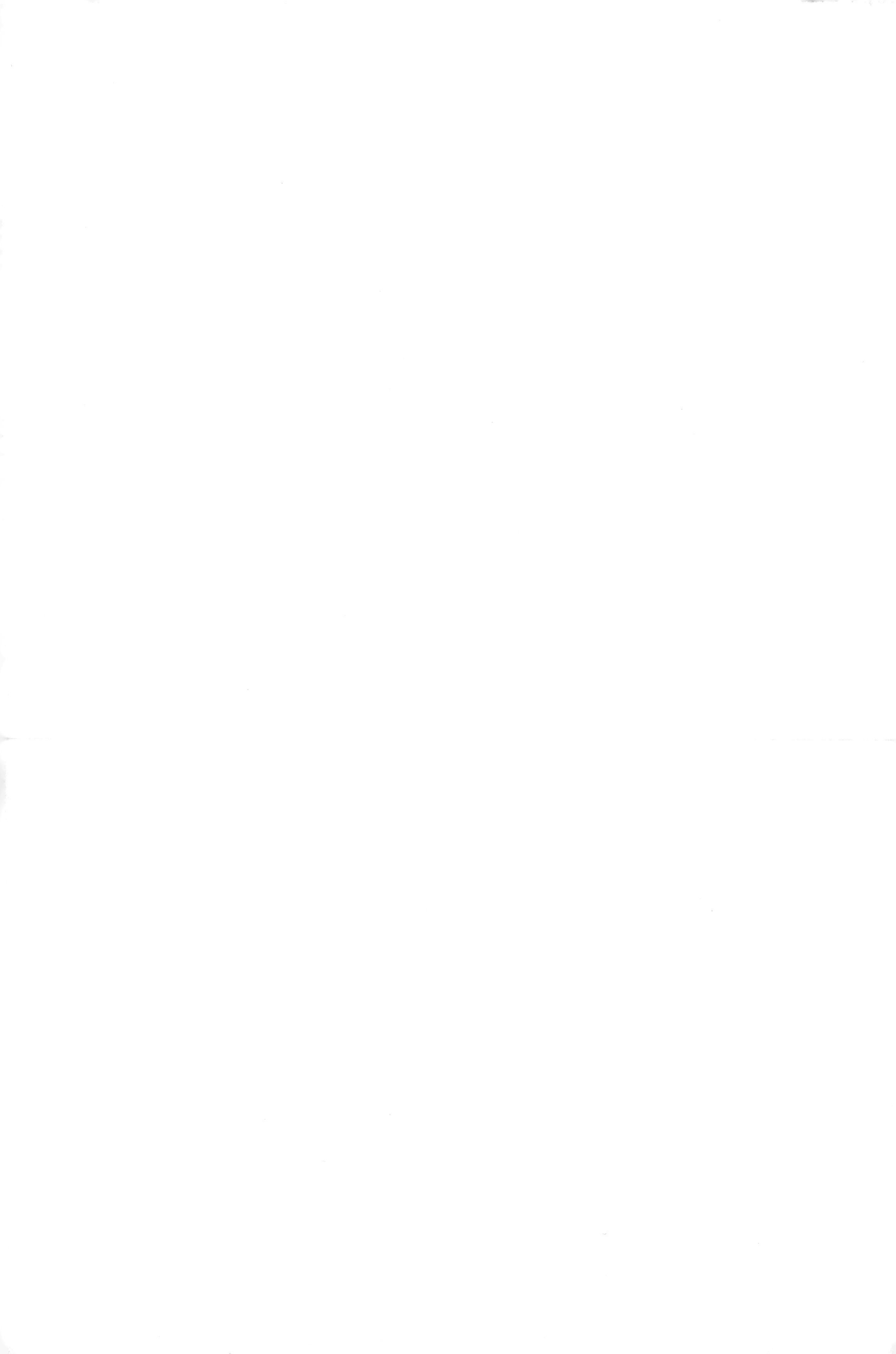